DELIVERANCE
of
LOVE, LIGHT AND TRUTH

Also by David Knight

Pathway

I am I: The Indweller of Your Heart

I am I: The Indweller of Your Heart (Part 2)

I am I: The Indweller of Your Heart (Part 3)

I am I: The Indweller of Your Heart 'Collection'

Leave the Body Behind-Sojourns of the Soul

A Pocket Full of God

DELIVERANCE
of
LOVE, LIGHT AND TRUTH

*CONTINUED CHANNELLED LOVE AND WISDOM
FROM THE TRANS-LEÁTIONS OF THE
TWO SISTERS STAR GROUP*

David Knight

Deliverance of Love, Light and Truth

Copyright © 2008 by DPK Publishing-AscensionForYou.
All rights reserved.
Previous ISBN-13: 978-1-4251-2447-2
This edition: ISBN 978-1-8380091-5-1

Updated Version Copyright © 2021
Printed in the United States of America.

Without limiting the rights under copyright reserved above, no part of this publication may be reproduced, stored in, or introduced into a retrieval system, or transmitted, in any form, or by any means (electronic, mechanical, photocopying, recording, or otherwise) without the prior written permission of both the copyright owner and the above publisher of this book.

This book is sold subject to the condition that it shall not, by way of trade or otherwise, be lent, resold, hired out, or otherwise circulated without the publisher's prior consent in any form of binding or cover other than that in which it is published and without a similar condition including this condition being imposed on the subsequent purchaser. Under no circumstances may any part of this book be photocopied for resale.

The advice or methods found within this book may not be suitable for everyone. It is sold and accepted with the understanding that neither the publisher nor the author is held responsible for the results acquired from the guidance in this 'work'. The author's intention is to solely offer his experiences and wisdom to aid your own search for truth and spiritual development and to enhance your emotional, physical, and mental well-being. Always seek medical advice from a doctor or physician.

A CIP catalogue record for this book is available from the British library.

2021 Cover layout / design by Nathan Dasco
Original 2008 cover image courtesy of Bruce Walker

If you enjoy reading **Deliverance of Love, Light and Truth** you can find further inspiring and motivational books when you join David's mission for a full and blissful life'.

To learn more, visit: www.AscensionForYou.com

CONTENTS

Foreword	9
Chapter 1: 'FROM THE ILLUSION & CONFUSION'	23
Chapter 2: 'FOREVER TO BE TRUE'	59
Chapter 3: 'CLEARING KARMA & THE THREE-FOLD FLAME'	81
Chapter 4: 'COLORS'	99
Chapter 5: 'LIGHT'	125
Chapter 6: 'COLLATING DATA SINCE THE DAWN OF TIME'	145
Chapter 7: 'A LIFE ... ALIVE'	159
Chapter 8: 'THE MIRACLE OF YOU'	169
Chapter 9: 'ENDEAVOR'	183
Endnotes	217
About the Author	223
Invitation from David Knight	225

ILLUSTRATIONS

Picture 1: THE SPACE GRID	11
Picture 2: THE EXPANDING FLAME OF LIGHT	32
Picture 3: THREE: WELCOME	61
Picture 4: THE BRIDGE TO AN OPEN-HEART	65
Picture 5: THE 'FOUR'	73
Picture 6: WITHIN THE THREE-FOLD FLAME	86
Picture 7: THE VIOLET FLAME AND THE HIGHER SELF	97
Picture 8: DIVINE LOVE TO ERASE DARKNESS AND HATE	116
Picture 9: LOVE FROM THE 'DIVINE'	117
Picture 10: A BLACK HOLE TO DISCOVER A GOAL	131
Picture 11: THE CRAFT	140
Picture 12: TWO PLANETS	142
Picture 13: LEATURUS AND THE TEMPLE	143
Picture 14: THE RADIATING COIL AROUND YOUR HEART	158
Picture 15: THE AKASHIC RECORDS	178
Picture 16: THE BUTTERFLY	196
Picture 17: THE SEA OF SOULS	198
Picture 18: GOLDEN RAIN OF LOVE	200
Picture 19: THE ASCENSION CONNECTION	201

ACKNOWLEDGEMENTS

To God, our Heavenly Father/Mother … our 'creator', I thank you from my heart for your immense love and light you bestow upon us all, and for this further opportunity to share so much of your strength and understanding. To the Trans-leátions, for without you and your connection through my heart and mind, then this second book would never have been collated. On this earth-plane, thank you to my wife Caroline, for your continued love and support and encouragement you have given to me, and your forgiveness … when I have been too busy to share my time with you. Thanks to my family and friends and everyone who has contributed to the book, especially Bruce (my friend and colleague) who reproduced the illustrations from my original channelled drawings.

MAY GOD BLESS YOU ALL

FOREWORD

The **Pathway** [1] to love and light around the world, has it been taken on board? Has it been digested 'within' to touch your heart and soul and mind? I could suggest that it has or is it just a coincidence that you have now picked up this book, the second 'work' from the Transleátions [2] of the Two Sisters Star Group?

Well, 'Deliverance' could mean many things to you. Perhaps it is a continuation of your own inner search for knowledge, wisdom and truth, or maybe you yearn for the answers to mankind's questions about life and creation … or simply wish to clear an emotional pain deep within your heart.

I believe there are both guidelines and solutions for every one of us contained inside this book, and the worry and fear we hold in our lives is going to be erased. The information it contains can solve much of our own confusion about why we are here and where we are heading. You may even find a picture or poem or the words you have been waiting for your whole life.

So, please let each page and chapter become a new opening or door to your true 'self', the inner reality and truth of 'you'. In this process try to let go of any preconceptions that you may have and allow your soul to feel the love and light which envelops your very being.

However, before you go on to read the introduction of this book, I'd like to share with you a vision and message from the Transleátions, for it helped me to understand that a further collation of information was to take place. This was another link to these angelic beings whom many describe as the 'grays' … a connection and alliance for us all.

Monday 8th January 1996

This occurred during a deep sleep. It began with me walking across a brilliant white 'room', and I approached what resembled a large 'viewing' screen. I instinctively knew this was a star map, a universal 'directory' (overlaid by pale blue grid lines) which highlighted both galaxies and constellations.

The space 'beyond' was the deepest, darkest black, interspersed with brilliant flashes of neon blue … radiating like an aura, spiralling outwards. PICTURE 1: THE SPACE GRID.

Suddenly, images of a Star system zoomed from left to right. As this occurred, a voice (as if in my mind), spoke of the 'Pleiades'. It was as if I was being made aware of a link with the Trans-leátions. Everything became blurred and I woke up.

My mind and heart raced, yet I felt frozen within the stillness of my bed. In contemplating the experience, the images in my mind rolled by over and over again, as if I was watching an old-fashioned cinefilm. The Star group I witnessed certainly did resemble the 'open' star cluster—the Pleiades [3]—which is in the constellation of Taurus.

Foreword

PICTURE ONE: THE SPACE GRID

Then ... bang, the revelation hit me! It was a clear message 'life' exists everywhere, and that we are all connected and truly 'one'!

A few weeks later on the 25th of January 1996, I received the following poem. I feel that it belongs right here and would like to share it with you. It is called,

Deliverance of Love, Light and Truth

SOMETHING NEW

To define life of the most peaceful, wondrous being,
Brings words of love ... to enter every living thing.
And with contrasting opinion's that divide your soul and mind,
There's a need to pull together, too know the truth of all mankind.

You have now been shown a door; and a Pathway clear and wide,
But have you 'opened' and accepted, or did you think it was a lie?
For the energy that flows ... contains its original trace,
To maintain and help you all ... the entire world and human race.

So, build the bridges of emotions, as new feelings cross the globe,
Lighting up in all directions, with your heart on sleeves to show.
To reflect and rise above, as new embers of the light,
And soar high and far and wide, for deep 'within' the soul takes flight.

For today is a new start, that each of you could make,
Consider there are no boundaries, only joy and bliss at stake?
In participation and togetherness, of every living thing,
To ascend the cord of light, and make it chime and sing.

So now you have begun, with this book and page-wide open,
But is it a mere gesture, and simply just a token?
And is becoming 'one', still the continued goal,
To live in peace and harmony ... to be kind unto your soul?

Now travel deep within, and hear these different words,
For this is really new, that no one else has seen or heard.
We hope it mends all hearts, which lay behind those darkened screens,
Be 'one' in love and light, and then define what can't be seen.

Foreword

Thursday 11th January 1996 (7:45 pm)

After the vision/message a few days ago, I knew it was time to pick up the pen again. Somehow, I felt a communication would be channelled for me to collate the Trans-leátions inner dictations of love and light and truth.

I sat and prayed for 'light' to surround and protect me from any disruptive influences. Then, I 'opened' myself to receive the vibrant connection to ask, "My dear family, friends, teachers, and guides, I know that you are here, yet I have missed you so much. Please help me to evolve and trust everything is as it should be, so I can progress and help others too. (There is so much on my mind, with decisions to make and other people's feelings I have to consider).

I long to write your words of love, friendship, and wisdom. Please, dear Trans-leátions, hear my call from my heart. Draw closer than ever before. You are so special and important to me. Help me to grow with your knowledge so that I may move forward and serve in the name of love and truth."

A few seconds must have passed, when suddenly a feeling of intense, pure energy seemed to flow over my body ... as if a wisp of silk had miraculously enveloped my being, protecting, and loving me. It was overwhelming. Such peace. I knew at this precise moment they were here again.

COMMUNICATION: *Oh, my son. We hear your cry from where you are, and it flies so far and wide that you could never know. Please understand, we are here when you need us ... and we will always be together.*

David, we see your problems and feel the emotions of your heart that soar so high and sometimes, so low. This is natural for human beings. You cannot hide it. You cannot deceive it from yourself. And, as you progress and grow, you will know and think of the right answers and become stronger too. This will enable you to cope with your experiences and move forward as you and your heart desires. Everything in good time.

What you are going through with higher frequencies—along with many other people who are coming to terms with an awakening of

Deliverance of Love, Light and Truth

their inner selves—is natural. Never force or try to change or push in the wrong direction. Your feelings can often be misguided, as there are always distractions. It is these things you must also understand too. It has been said before, and you know what is meant by, 'Do not fight what is inevitable.'

You also realize that we do not mean to fight by hand or knife or gun but describe only the struggle within yourself. So, it is very important to accept your intuition, and by trusting this you will then trust your 'self'. This will make you stronger to cope with life and with the things that can make so many of you feel 'down'.

Comprehend the light is always there but can seem shielded by someone else's thoughts or by the 'in built' confusion we have described before. Also, sow the seeds of love, for that is all you need to do. And stop, (if you can), trying to expect too much from yourself. Let things flow my son and you will get to where you want and where you are meant to be.

In your meditation earlier today, you experienced the colors [4] we had revealed for you. You chose them because they resonated the brightest for you at this time. None are classed as 'better' than another, as each have their own different tasks and abilities. Know they will provide additional strength and they will assist you in the near future.

You will also feel there is the need to help other people, and there are many ways and avenues to do this. Each form of service has its own merits, and therefore once again, go with the flow of your heart and love. Please appreciate time and effort is a sacrifice itself, even if you do something different to someone else. Each to their own, for the creator does not judge in the sense of better or worse on an issue of service or loving others.

Sometimes, people think their tasks are hidden, and yet they are not ... though there can be many energies around you all which influence—or at least try to trick or take you away from the desired goal, sometimes deliberately. This can be part of the individual's learning process. It is for the person to make up their own mind (which may not be easy), but your own future and the future of others depends upon it. Is this message a burden or a helping hand? Remember we love you all. This is always so, and no matter how

Foreword

difficult or demanding something is, you are never, ever alone!

So, keep going as you are on the right track. Do not ever look back. Your destiny lays outstretched before you with a golden glow and shining light from heaven ... and such love resides inside (and for) every form of life. Peace, love, truth, and harmony are your birthright and lies within the grasp of all.

We would also like you to remember that when someone does not follow their true purpose, they not only hurt themselves but also those around them too. Appreciate a mistake is not a mistake if you learn from it. How many 'teachers' have said this throughout history and of course in ours too! Therefore, we ask for everyone to release both doubt and fear ... and erase everything that does not feel right in your lives. You can then take the flight to the bliss that is waiting for you. The choices are yours, and yours alone. What decision will you make to fulfill your destiny?

David be strong. You will come through everything you have described to us at the start of these 'communications', and of what is in your heart and mind too. Those who read or listen to these words, please know the life that lays ahead of you may seem many years ... yet in reality is but a flicker of time and light. Understand it is what each of you do with this that determines whom, what and where you become ... to be 'one'? Simply trust and love and you will be okay.

David, we would now link back to 'PATHWAY' once more. For once the book is published, greater progress can be made for you and many others too. New doors will continue to open and there will be new ideas and challenges too. But, with your hand on your heart and your heart in the light, you will then be carried forward on each dull or bright day or night.

Your divinity is there for other's to witness and this is your new concern. People may laugh or cry at what you undertake and complete in your 'service'. Yes, to serve the great 'Spirit' as everyone does in their many ways. We are all individuals, but ultimately, we're on the same inner pathway to serve both love and light and nothing can distract or weaken that.

So, when things have settled down a little more in your work and home life, then we will start the second book, these new 'works'. Yet

Deliverance of Love, Light and Truth

another beginning, but a continuance too. It has now been decided to let you know there will be new things no one else on the earth-plane has ever heard of or even seen ... and these will soon materialize. A sharing of wisdom and knowledge and pictures too will make many people gasp, hunger, and thirst for more information and for further directions to progress.

Please know that the text of this book will be longer than Pathway, and we hope as well-received by those who have opened their hearts and minds to fresh ways of thinking, living and loving. The name of this book will have a universal meaning. It will have a single word as its title, but it shall contain a message underneath. You can all interpret this in many ways.

At this point, the name of the new book flashed through my mind!

COMMUNICATION(Cont.): *You pause David because you are unsure that you have the correct name of the title. This is okay, pause again and let this picture flow through you. Do not fight against the words. It is 'DELIVERANCE: OF LOVE, LIGHT AND TRUTH'. Yes indeed, love and light and truth ... delivered through you!*

The design of the front cover of this book will be left to you. We read your thoughts and you are thinking of bright colors ... not unlike a rainbow within the depths of space and new birth. Use your heart, for there you will find all that you will need.

We need to go now, but you will sense when it is time to communicate again. Some spare 'time' and also a little reward is on its way. Yes, a little payday to help you along.

Trust in us as you always have done until you are 'home' (that day we spoke privately of) in the light, become 'ONE' my son. Peace to all as always. We are forever watching over you. Bless you. Keep going and be strong. Goodbye.

Thank you so much. You have given me more than you can ever know and of the day when I return, I will not ask to speed along. Though it is difficult to find the right words, all I can say is that you are in my heart and soul ... and my light and energy are always here for you.

I wish to share this information and your love for the world. I also want to share my life, together with this knowledge for each soul to grow. My heart, my door is always open to you. Bless you. Praise to the 'great white Spirit', our God ... our creator.

Saturday 16th January 1996

Hey, I've won £72.20 at the football pools! This is the first time I've ever won on them ... which I supposed is to help with the cost of materials like paper and pens etc. Thank you, it is much appreciated!

Saturday 27th January 1996

Over the last few days, I'd been wondering when the next communication would arrive. I didn't have to wait too long!

Sunday 28th January 1996

Dear Trans-leátions, thank you for the dream last night and for the 'Two-Sisters' symbol [5] so I would know it was time to pick up the pen. I offer my love and light for truth and for guidance for us all. A continued path of information ... a continued 'Deliverance'. Milanderer and Zerrog [6] my dear friends and family, please may the pen now flow so that others are also able to grow.

COMMUNICATION: *Welcome again, David. The dream we had sent was a signal to send you another message, but you seem surprised ... and this surprises us! You were right in your interpretation and a similar theme it will always take to help you personally know what needs to be done and the route to take.*

Okay, what we are about to discuss will also be part of the introduction to 'Deliverance'. We wish to lay the foundations for this new book, but before we start, we know of your concerns regarding the workload ahead and what lies in store for you. Everything will be fine.

Deliverance of Love, Light and Truth

 Please know that part of the earnings (spiritually or materialistically) from 'Pathway' and this new book is part of the gift to sustain your home life. It will also enable you to continue in this line of work and help others seek the light for the greater good. We reiterate that you are the only person on the earth-plane to receive us and this will remain so. Only others can say whether this is a burden, or an immense love and beauty, a challenge bestowed.

 A major part of your life is truly underway, and this can assist many other light-workers in saving the day. This is required for the greater goal and work that lies ahead. To enable you to share and send love to those in need and to dispel and cast out the crime, the hate, and the greed.

 In essence, the progression of many souls shall produce the stillness needed to experience the core divinity of the creator, so this responsibility is not yours alone. Every person can assist in producing a layer of vibration and energy that connects to the cord of light for Ascension.

 At the same time this pen flows, we do not know how many people on the earth-plane will actually know of our name or where we are from. But what we do know is that those who read and understand the first communications will already acknowledge the love inside their hearts. Or, they have now crossed the bridge of doubt which had stood before them ... to open their souls to a new direction of thinking, feeling, and being.

 Please know we are here for each race, creed, nation, and color of skin, to every one of your next of kin. We also feel this 'Deliverance' will be what you make it to be. It can be a new path—behind that previously closed door—which can now lead you forward. Or perhaps it can be something that keeps you in place, yet still makes you sit up, to think and wonder and light up your face.

 We're intrigued and would like to ask, "Do you leave the door open so others may see and learn? Or do you close the door behind you to hide from the unknown?" In the course of true events, the routes each individual take are but a fleeting glimpse of a new spec of light, time, and space.

 As this is so, acquaintances will notice and see the difference in you. Hopefully, they will also follow the same truth that resides inside

Foreword

every soul ... where <u>all</u> answers are found. It is down to the individual whether the door was closed, and stays closed, or if they now open their heart to reveal their own path of reality.

As long as you are true to yourself it does not really matter, because it is only when you deny acceptance of your higher self the confusion can set in ... which can intentionally (or unintentionally) blind others own perception. Therefore, we hope this new road can help people progress and avoid a return to what they have previously always known, living life by what was told or mislead you all to believe.

Comprehend the light can work in mysterious and unbelievable ways to help you along. So, when you read and take in some information and knowledge of these new communications you may not understand it, but in time, you will.

To start with, we aim to convey the implications of 'Self' denial and this will move on to the acceptance and harmonization from the inside and out. We shall then move on to the collaboration and development between your earth-plane and other worlds.

From there, we'll advance to the beauty and life that lies ahead in the coming years, with the joining of the 'cords of light' in more detail than has been described before. In addition, we shall also explain and reveal in pictures, 'scenes' that will make your heart glow or sink, depending on how you feel ... and of course upon how you really think.

There really is so much to look forward to David ... with messages and poems, joy and laughter and tears of love are coming through to you all. Overall, this will be a continued and sustained growth. With the openness of your heart, soul, and mind it will bring success and emanate the love and light around your beautiful planet.

Okay, today's communication is due to end, but we will conclude the introduction next time. We will also deliver the first chapter soon. Perhaps you will consider the title of the first chapter yourself. Maybe it will come to you by reading over these notes? We love you always and watch intently over your new growth and expansion. We are always forever to be 'one'. Goodbye, in peace and in truth from me.

Bless you, all, from my heart. Thank you.

Sunday 19th February 1996

I awoke at 7.07 am from several dreams ... relaying a clear indication to link again with the Trans-leátions. I couldn't wait to be 'still' tonight and feel their energy and love drawing close to me. It was approximately 8.20 pm when this next communication came through.

COMMUNICATION: *Hello once again my precious son. Our connection is so clear that you can now feel the touch of my hand on your right shoulder. You are correct in regard to the energy that you feel, and how the candle flame also lights up your page to write with a resurgence of our love.*

Having heard your plea, know you will always be near to thee. We are proud of you for the work that you do. You have worked hard in the preparation of 'PATHWAY' and Sheila [7] has too. Tell her from us, "God bless you, for the love that is strong in your heart."

In contrast, we witness through our 'eyes of light' that there has been little improvement [8] within the cords of love that progress across your globe. We will not shout out aloud, but gently ask, "What are you all doing, the one and the crowd"? We know and understand people are trying—and make no mistake of that—but we observe the darkness and hate which and attempts to distort the energy of truth and peace.

Therefore, these words of wisdom, along with other books that are being collated from— and with—other planes [9] and worlds by different sources will be needed to change so much.

More people are required to open their closed hearts and minds a little more, or maybe far and wide! This will let in the surge of beautiful energy, resembling a typhoon or hurricane that swirls high above the land ... whilst touching many a shore like the oceans upon the earth. We will be with you all to lend this helping hand but ask everyone to try much harder to succeed in peace and harmony.

Okay, growth and expansion is to continue, and we hope it is never in vain. Will this be the next step or journey inside the mind or relate to another existence, dimension and 'plane'? We understand it can be so hard to distance yourselves from your

Foreword

everyday lives but the call has begun and the road is set before you now.

One's decision to envisage this as being vast or narrow in which to manoeuvre is yours and yours alone to make. So, stretch out beyond the senses to touch the brilliance of your consciousness. When you are 'still', you can push back the walls of despair and also forget all your cares. The way forward can reveal itself and allow the light to feed and nourish your heart.

Indeed, by <u>embracing the route</u> you identify the goal, the reconnection of your very being and purpose of your beautiful soul. Just keep going and don't ever look back. You are the creator's love, so abort the crowded track. Remember, old feelings are only a product of the past ... held within the mind. Comprehend you are all 'one' of a kind, born of light pre-sent from the dawn of awakening.

So, precious children of light ... continue on your new path so you can shine more brightly. Never, ever doubt what is in 'store', for here is all you have ever experienced and so much more.

'Deliverance' is a page of your life's book and when you have read and filled your heart with this 'work'; your friends and guides will begin to notice the changes within you. They will see if it has been gently taken on board or whether you feel you have been coerced by hook or by crook. We hope it's not the latter.

Know this would not be a physical or mental force to push and hurry you, but more a gentle opening or tug of your heartstrings which will enable you to pull and rip apart your life's mystery and its false, dark curtain of doubt and fear.

OK, now read on and reflect upon these and many other things, with anticipation and a desire to start anew with hope and enthusiasm for a new life. Perhaps this will continue to strengthen your faith or help you embark upon a total change of direction, even a life's dedication? Here is a poem, and we hope it will help you to return to some action, for deep inside it may cause some reaction.

Deliverance of Love, Light and Truth

MOVING ON ... BE 'ONE'

*Children, dear children of love and light,
Carry the flame ... but do not hold any blame.
Now come to the creator though never in vain,
As love, light, and truth, will always, always rein.*

*A promise and a sacrifice that we have made to date,
To never leave you early, even if it is too late.
Nor to worry you or place you all in shame,
As we are one together, for deep inside we're just the same.*

*Your experience could be turbulent, with your life so full of yearning,
But we hope to carry you through, the lessons and you're learning.
So, we trust you open up, and proceed take this book,
Your mind to read and digest ... your heart to see and look.
Take not it's real face value, but to find the inner test,
The truth inside you'll follow, 'till your 'one' at peace and rest.*

Well, David, Chapter One is to begin and this is where you are asked to step in ... it's title to decide. This will come from your heart, perhaps a name or a line to lead you away from the dark. A clue for you and a helping hand, and a touch from us to indicate the new 'home' ... a true promised land.

So, goodbye for now. Please, continue the work and be ready for the pen to flow again when another dream is sent. Our love, peace and truth are always here for you all.

Bless you all. My love to you is forever from my heart.

CHAPTER ONE: 'FROM THE ILLUSION ... AND CONFUSION'

Saturday 9th March 1996

I have decided to call this chapter 'From the Illusion ... and confusion', but why? Well, it is because there seems there's so very much of this in our lives. However, before we move forward there is something I would like to share with you all. It is a painful experience, and yet full of 'love'.

This is quite strange for at the end of Pathway (book one) we had discussed the pain and suffering in the loss of a loved one, be it a relative, friend or perhaps even a family 'pet'. I had stated that these events in your life can break your heart in two yet could also be part of your karma which affects those around you too.

Tonight, my wife and I discovered from a neighbor that our beautiful white kitten 'Moosey' (who had been missing), had been killed on the main road near our home. Through everything I have experienced with knowledge of life and death (rebirth) I was not prepared for the unbearable pain and ache inside me when we buried him and said our goodbyes. Why do we have such grief when we know he is in God's care, in 'his' love and light?

How I slept I do not know, but I did find my higher-self and dream guides and teachers who tried to help me understand. One of the dreams involved the Trans-leátions and contained personal information of 'life' and the transference to the 5th 'Dimension'. [10] (Which was to help me cope).

In another dream, some small trees in a garden were blown over and stripped bare which were symbolizing life and our emotions being stripped of love. I knew I had to stand them up, for them to be strong.

Deliverance of Love, Light and Truth

I needed to repair them, as these reflected our broken hearts.

I awoke with tears in my eyes for I was overcome with emotion, both in my mind and in my heart. I then heard clairaudiently [11] a soft and gentle voice who then slowly began to sing, "For ... I ... can't ... help ... falling in love with ... you." I felt as if there was an angelic presence beside me and Elvis Presley's words and song of love were to comfort me. I had always felt—and few people would disagree with me— that his voice and songs were indeed made in 'Heaven'.

I lay still in bed. Is this a loss or a weakness to overcome? Perhaps it's a fault, or strength that I/we do not understand? Maybe this is a point in our lives when we should not doubt our faith or in God's love? It is for this reason I have shared this with you. Perhaps the very next 'communication' can help one of you too.

Sunday Night 10th March 1996 (7.15 pm)

Heavenly Father/Mother God, my Spirit guides, teachers and the Trans-leátions, thank you all for your love and also for my dreams last night which let me know to 'open' once again as a channel for the spoken words. Please protect me while I am 'still' and allow your light to shine for the entire world to see.

Please help and guide us for you know what has occurred over the last few days. Such pain at the loss of 'Moosey', our dear kitten, who was so much more than a friend to us. This pain and hurt run so deep that we cannot eat or sleep. Why, after all I've learned and come to know (with your guidance) do I breakdown so?

I am here to serve, and I am helping Caroline the best I can with your truth and love and support. Please help us through these difficult times. Let me know what you want to say, to continue with the 'Deliverance'. Bless you, all. My heart aches so much. Please help our love go to 'Moosey' too.

COMMUNICATION: *Oh, my son, my dear son, what has begun ... has begun. All of your tears are so beautiful. They are tears of golden love and light, and we have seen many of them flow these last few days and nights.*

From the Illusion ... and Confusion

We would like to say to you that we 'understand' but that is not fair to you both. We know your love is strong and you will succeed in going over this sometimes-insurmountable fence. Make no mistake; your love illuminates like a beacon with the most beautiful 'rays' of light. These radiate as an everlasting Star, which shines both from here and there and also from afar. While you both weep and cry the creator has spoken in truth ... even though you often ask the 'Why?'

What happened was meant to be. An 'experience' for you both ... and for 'Moosey' too. Though nothing can ever take away the love you have shared and still do, and never worry, he loves you both and always will too.

He waits and stays in the beautiful light, and he did not feel any pain as he took God's 'flight'—a super express train to the heavenly realms above. He is safe and has many friends and now plays with many children on the plane of existence where he now resides. Know that Moosey watches you too, as you sit still, and also when you lay down and cry.

People may think this is a trick of words because a cat cannot think or feel, but they are mistaken. He can do so much more than these things. He can 'love' and has a heart and a wonderful gift of sharing what he has been given by the creator—a light source and soul which is his very being and essence.

Dear Caroline, David is right, for we indeed have a message for you. We hope it will lift your heart, even for a short while for your tears that now fall could overflow the earth's river Nile. Precious, child of light, you cry and wonder of the 'why' don't you? You sit and miss what you think you have lost, but pray my child because you have not, nor will you at any cost. We can see and feel your heart has a void ... an emptiness you believe can never be made complete, but please open your heart and mind my daughter ... my child of light.

Fill your mind with the good things you shared together, and everything will be okay ... because, beyond doubt, he knows you love and still care for him. We have seen with our own eyes, and he is safe within the love and light. When you feel so down and wish the world to swallow you up, just lift your heart to the creator's loving and overflowing cup. Then 'drink', not through the physical

Deliverance of Love, Light and Truth

body, but quench your thirst for wisdom, knowledge and for the love that appears to rip you in two.

You have so much love 'within' you, and you only need to let it show so you can understand the truth ... to grow. Know you will receive a dream/message when it is the right time for you. This will help and give you a chance to comprehend what also lays ahead.

We now ask you a question. At this very second of your life, what is it that you would wish for—more than anything in the world? To see and hold and kiss your beloved cat? You will do these things we promise you. You only need to open and release the clenched grip around your heart. By doing so, your love flows to the one thing that you believe you miss and then you will experience that precious kiss and gift.

The last thing we would like to say on this is that the minutes and hours and days— as you perceive it—will seem to slowly pass by. However, when things have settled down, you will appreciate time is irrelevant other than in your world ... because when you see him again, it will seem like you have never been apart— such is the power of the creator's love which bonds and connects us all together. So, precious child of light, sleep well tonight. Rest with an open heart and touch the love inside you, for everything will be okay.

David, as in previous chapters of Pathway, you have learned and grown and everything you have experienced these past few days is the same process. Yes, it has been painful. But isn't this ironic, for you had once said that you had not experienced a loss of such love. Have you now not come full circle?

What occurred is also an experience for and of the many ... to observe and listen to their own heart's flames [12] as they came together from their short separation. Let us remind everyone on the earth-plane, it is not just the physical body that can feel, touch or sense love. So do not despair ... just care.

Remember ... everything resides in the light, and even darkness cannot exist without it. The creator's love is for you all, please realize this. David, there has been a question that has flashed through your mind. Please write it down.

From the Illusion ... and Confusion

It's just, right now, how I feel inside when I cry (and when we cry together), and also all those who have lost their children, their loved ones or beloved pets. How do we all cope?

COMMUNICATION: *Unconditional love my son. Though love is internal, it is displayed 'outwardly' in many forms as we have said before. Every one of you has different 'love', but some love appears weaker or stronger than others. No one holds any blame and there should never be any shame. Not for—or from— you, or indeed anyone else.*

You are how you are all made to be, an expression of God through the choices you each make in this particular lifetime of learning and experience. Make no mistake, you are individuals and every person is different in their own unique ways. And yet, you are all the same divine sparks within your 'core' (or soul) ... 'one' energy linked together by fragments of love and light from the creator.

So, you will both cope as long as you hold onto the truth. Turn 'within' as often as you can. We know that the emotional pain can be grotesque as if the darkest hour of your fears attempt to steal your breath ... but turn to the light and this will diminish. You will then grow stronger in the recognition we are together, forever.

Okay, you must allow your heart's flame to rise David, and become rebalanced with our own. Now trust in the power of light, and we'll overcome all struggles to succeed with the love, wisdom, and knowledge you require, and this will bring you through life's difficulties from which you will never tire.

'Go with the flow' and feel the creator's energy which flows and spirals from you to those in need. Remember, it is not only those with a stethoscope who are needed to make the heart stop the bleed, because you all have the gifts inside you to succeed ... if you utilise them correctly. Therefore, go with what seems right for you, as circumstances will prevail too.

We now ask, how many of you feel trapped in a certain or particular situation? Who or what has caused this emotion? Is it you who has prevented yourself from being who you can become? Know you are already free to make those life choices that connect with the reality of being 'you'. Therefore, be what you want to be, and if it is in the name of truth ... then so shall it be written before the eternal witness.

To conclude, proceed with an open heart and believe we are here for you. Caroline, bless you for your love, though sometimes it remains hidden. Remember, 'Moosey' sends his love to you but in this pain, you cannot see or feel it. So, push away all notions of regret to hear his 'meow' and purr, (just as you remember him) and a beautiful white kitten will be with thee.

Every day is a new beginning and can also be an end. Therefore, lift up your hearts once more we say, for the 'future' is only your tomorrow from the seeds you plant today. As we finally reiterate, please come to the creator's love. All of you come and knock upon...

HEAVEN'S DOOR

Push it open, push it wide,
Peep inside and never hide.
All to learn and all to grow,
You are God's children, in a heavenly glow.
So be still and calm and look for love it's a must,
Just believe in the light and in the divine ... always trust.

This message now draws to a close, so wait for another day before picking up the pen. Know these words are for you to decide where to place them, either in the introduction or within chapter One. Please look to the 'Heavens' for the true light and 'gold', for this is within you all, your true 'home'. Until the next time we 'meet', goodbye for now, in love, truth and peace from us all.

Saying thank you does not convey my feelings. How can I describe the energy, the peace, and the love I sense when our frequencies connect? My heart had felt as if it was broken in two, but now it feels that it's been put back together, with a magical glue ... made from your love! To anyone who is grieving at this time, I truly hope this communication can also mend your aching, breaking heart.

From the Illusion ... and Confusion

Tuesday 19th March 1996

I pray to the great white spirit, our God/ creator and to the Transleátions, please let this pen flow, so that the entire world may grow and know. Help us with your love and advice to overcome our daily problems and life's tests we all face ... and for spiritual guidance and education too. Bless you, all, your son of light, David.

COMMUNICATION: *Bless you too my son. As the frequency of your open heart settles down to receive the information, and as the candle flame rises to help you 'see', realize we are here to help every living thing turn 'within' and witness their own divinity.*

Sometimes, your shoulders appear to buckle from the heaviness pouring from the mind ... these burdens of ones emotions and the struggle of life itself. It does not have to be this way if you stop for a short while to remain 'still'. All the direction and love you need resides <u>within</u> your inner peace.

Please know that the creator's love is infinite. It never diminishes and will never leave you suspended or high and dry, even when you lay down to sob and cry. There is so much to learn, but you must all understand there is no end where knowledge and wisdom are concerned.

David, we are glad you spent time last night presiding over the written word ... and you have named chapter one well. The two main words you have used leave and pose a massive question to the reader or listener. They encompass a wide range of feelings both inside and out, but are illusion and confusion one of the same, or are they both to blame?

The time has come for everyone to embrace their development of their souls, but what does this entail for both the individual and for the masses? Can there ever be a single gift, prayer or poem that can sustain and carry you all through the web of deceit, hate, lies and the darkness? What really leads the child/ pupil and the teacher (and so-called master) astray?

Understand these traits are a pretense ... merely hurdles to overcome as you progress (in strength) to jump over each challenge as a fence. The obstacles you all face are both simple to explain and easy to diffuse, but they are also not to be misused. Indeed, it is your innate struggle with the mind and ego over the perception of one's self-realization.

Let us take an example of a wandering soul on a journey. It could be a man, woman, or child who has packed their bags and embarked upon the enlightenment trail. Over mountains, they climb to reach for the 'Son', but what knowledge and wisdom do they unearth of the 'one'? The route now continues over river, land, and sea ... in search of the real 'him', and the real 'me'. They look, and they search for one day they will know, come around now full circle, for only self that does grow. In discovering themselves a glorious true find, the process of life must be played out to find.

Why have so many of you gone on this mysterious journey to search and explore when all along the answers have been elsewhere since the beginning of time. The real journey begins and ends with you ... and the real connection and exploration it brings to the one and only true 'source'. Only 'inside' you are the sights that you could not dream of or comprehend. Turning within is the answer, for true 'insight'.

David, in the last three years you have witnessed some immense visions and precognitions and experienced many emotions. You have also journeyed where no human has gone before, and yet all of this is not even a fraction, the slightest spec of the divine and creation.

What does this imply to the masses? Well, people may feel downhearted and left behind in their mind's perception, but we say do not worry or feel this way. Perhaps some will be concerned with a lack of 'time' in their physical life, but as we explained earlier, nowhere else is there the importance placed upon it as you (humankind) do. We therefore say, do not be concerned, because when the Ascensions [13] has been completed, 'time' will be of no relevance to anyone or anything!

No doubt, some will still be confused, but as their hearts are opened and their minds expanded, they will be ready to move all obstacles to one side and then move forward in both comprehension and learning.

David, we would like you to try to draw the second picture of this book for it is relevant to be seen and interpreted by those who gaze

From the Illusion ... and Confusion

upon it. Please rest the pen for a few moments and comprehend the human race is like billions of candle. It is such a wonderful sight to see you all from both near and afar. Look into the flame of your heart and describe your experience.

As this picture came through me, I felt a burst of energy all around my body with a pulsating pressure around my 3rd eye/mind's eye. I could sense and feel flames and yet I knew they were souls of love and light, resembling glowing candles. It was like tower blocks of 'life' were rising from a mountaintop. Symbolically, they were all becoming the final cord of luminosity ... that will reach out and expand from the Earth to completely envelop the world with beautiful rings and radiating coils of light! Wonderful! (N.B.: I felt that I needed to call this, PICTURE TWO: 'THE EXPANDING FLAME OF LIGHT'.)

COMMUNICATION: *Draw these pictures so that people will see for themselves. It must be known that a universal ray of love & light will push aside everything that's misunderstood about their connection to the divine. This will cleanse the blood of the body, and the mind/consciousness too, for energy will not be decayed in any way, shape, or form. Everything will be pure and whole for those to embark on the 'wave' of their destiny. Will this wave of Ascension be a goodbye wave to those who are still yet to learn and grow?*

Imagine for a moment that you are stranded in dense fog, be careful where you tread or you just might get lost! Forwards, backwards or sideways will you go, and in each direction what will you learn and discover to know?

PICTURE TWO: 'EXPANDING FLAME OF LIGHT'

This haze is like frosted glass. Lean forward and press your face and nose against it. Is it real, or imaginary? Can you really feel it? Is it real and strong, or fake ... an illusion that has gone before in a previous lifetime's wake?

Now take a step ... or even a leap of faith and pierce this mist with your conviction and fortitude. You will not need to kick or punch it with a fist because the reality of you is all you need to reveal your real vision and bear witness to the true growth of your 'Self', an inner seed. Take another step without any trepidation of where to place your feet. Just glide each foot with strength from your heart to the clearing that now lies before you.

It has been there forever ... since 'time' immemorial, but only now can you accept the wonder and splendor of this heavenly glow, to finally comprehend through the belief that was sown. Appreciate the invisible screen that separates and diversifies you and your many

From the Illusion ... and Confusion

lives is as thick and hazy or as clear and thin as you will know 'within'. This will only be discovered when you have made the light your permanent home.

What we describe to you is but a glimpse of the truth that you may or may not know of. It has always been up to you to embark upon the voyage of discovery. The individual must wish to learn and not spurn the opportunities that present themselves each day ... indeed it is your 'Pathway' and 'Deliverance' to the everlasting goal and home. We will not command or lay down 'rules' for a single one of you ... ultimately, your success is determined only by you all. Each soul and heart and mind can stick with the illusion and your physical requirement's or you can knock the confusion for 'six' and make the start for the home run. Believe us when we say, in the pursuit of your realization you will have laughter and so much more fun.

That said, what we are about to explain is not meant to focus upon so-called negativity or to give additional energy to it either. However, we know many people who are suffering emotionally and mentally and physically with their hearts ripped open at their recent personal 'loss'. We hope our words may help them, even in a small way.

To all the families in Dunblane [14] and those families and relatives in Manila [15], inside of you is heavenly light which radiates the peace of the creator. Of your grief and pain that seems hard to comprehend, know there is 'one' who does. However, at this time of mourning, some of you might not believe what we wish to convey to you.

Please know your children, your teacher, and people are all safe ... and they will remain part of you, forever. Inside your hearts center you can feel, touch, and hold them again. You just need to push the 'illusion' to one side and begin to acknowledge that who and what you grieve for is not the end.

You will see them again, I promise you. They have not been 'lost' forever and they shall never be. Like David and Caroline earlier, you may well ask the 'why?' until your passing day. This question will never be far away from your thoughts, but if you place it within the deepest core of your hearts ... then the light will give you the answers you need. Memories sometimes fade but love is eternal, and

Deliverance of Love, Light and Truth

this is why you will be able to cope and live once again in the joy of their memory and being.

Remember too, that 'memory' is only a word. Please replace it with existence instead, because 'life' is infinite and rebirth a sacrifice. But for who? For them, their family, their friends, their mother, and father and for you all! We only want to say that love is everywhere but you will never know of the karmic 'slate' each soul (that crosses over) has chosen whilst you remain on the earth-plane. Pray, and in your prayers please trust in God. Then, turn within to the stillness and peace that resides there, for their love is constant and remains inside you too.

Time is drawing near for the pen to stop today. Some of you who have read those last few pages may think this a sad and painful note to end upon. Only on the outer mind is this so, for inside is a joy of love that can never be erased.

'Life' is complex if you make it so, but in true living, life can be simple. People may retort, "That is easy for you to say, you are not going through our blackest hour, this nightmare and hell!" Please understand, we have gone through all this and much more beyond your human experiences. Within us, the creator has installed an access route to the 'stillness' that is required to be understood and known for each and every moment that arises. (We will explain more about this at a later date in more detail.)

So, the 'Illusion and Confusion' must be stemmed and pushed aside to reveal the truth from 'self' inside. We will help and carry on with this assistance and move in this direction next time in our communication. David, bless you for the outpouring of your love through this pen today. As always, we'll be in touch to show and to trust. Keep going, and share love from your heart. Peace and joy to you all.

Thank you for drawing close today. Bless you, dear Transleátions and all my guides, teachers, family and friends on every plane of existence I have known, do know and will know. Your son of light, David.

Saturday 23rd March 1996 (12.15 pm)

Thank you for the dream you sent last night. I felt it represented what is happening to me emotionally and mentally and encompassed the things I've been through too.

I know I must view my surrounding circumstances with greater clarity to discover what my life experiences are revealing to me. Indeed, I must be strong, not weak and in the creators love and light, must always 'seek'.

Please help and advise us as there must be many people who face difficulties right now in their lives. I realise we must all continue to turn within to find true peace and direction as we have discussed many times before, however, if there is time today, can you continue with a short passage for this chapter? I only have 30 minutes before I need to leave for work. Huh! The so-called relevance of time in our world again!

COMMUNICATION*: Hello once again my son. As you feel the rush of energy and peace you know love and light are here and of course, it always will be.*

We ask you David, to think and learn from the dream we sent to you last night. It has a special meaning that you need to judge for yourself regarding the way to live your life. Hurt and pain can appear to manifest through the exterior but everything, all conditions and emotions materialize from the interior from what you think and feel, so peel off the outer coating and shed your 'skin' and reveal the beauty and love within.

Desire, lust and love can go hand in hand, but you all have to experience the inevitable choices that come within a 'band' of gold or a false ring of steel that traps and holds down what you really feel. Everything so tough, but is it all too much? Learn to live and learn to trust and feel the creator's immense loving touch that has been placed 'inside' you all.

No one can judge another or say who is a fool. Appreciate love is simple, not complex. It is not a workable and manipulative tool. The confusion in many hearts is really just a minute, single part. However entangled the complicated mesh of life becomes, the task is to unravel the threads of truth. Do not say, "What the heck' or "What the hell", but consider each individual scenario. You will then decide from inside, for it is there the hearts story will be told.

David, we have so much for you to write about but you have been busy this morning and we know what you mean regarding your time. As soon as you are ready to let it flow, then the pen will write for you and all will know. Carry on with your daily tasks and listen to both your outer and inner feelings. Then ask, 'Are they loud and make a din, or does the truth then become a sin?'

Do not feel down by that last line. It is just a reiteration of the choices you have to make because they will affect what goes on from a soon to be day and date. Continue the same route or decide to go another way ... we will always be with you, no matter what you decide.

Remember to think and feel for yourself, so come on stop sitting on that shelf! Make up your mind and get on with this life, only judging yourself will cut emotions with a knife. To chop and change reflects a drifting mind, so be 'one' ... together into the light, each and every day and night. Imagine and believe and then feel your destiny and help create the same sense of purpose for those who will listen and who are close to you too. Stay on course not to alter or be misled, but live life to the full, to the light beyond the non-physical 'dead'

We hope to carry on with much more, to come once again upon your shore. 'Till then we say may love, peace and truth be with you on this day. Goodbye, my son.

Thank you all from my heart. I know we will never part. So until our communication is connected within, love to you all, always and forever you are my brethren.

Monday 25th March 1996 (9.30 pm)

(After prayers). Please forgive me for I've been so tired. Yesterday I had not become 'still' to receive your channelled message and inner dictations of your love and light. I am still so exhausted ... drained both physically and emotionally but I pray and know the strength and love of the creator are all around ... which fills me both inside and out, to carry on and not to complain or shout.

Please let the frequencies now connect once again to move and communicate through this pen. I now feel the energy and the vibrations increasing and so dearly wish to let the world know that we are 'one'.

During this special time today, I must mention my sadness at what is going on within the animal kingdom right now and humankind's proposed slaughter of as many as eleven million cows. Is this a sacrifice beyond comprehension to justify our destructive intention? Please let this flow so altogether we can grow.

COMMUNICATION: *We are so glad you are able to be close again little one, (my son), to let these words come through the 'planes' of existence and vibrations of frequency that many will and one day know. We are here and all around you. We also keep you safe and sound and while you watch the candle flame rise, the energy and peace are there for your heart and also for you all. As it rises 6, 8, 10 inches (ca. 25 cm) or more the heat intensifies and so the wax drops. Now, as you draw in even closer it starts to pour, just like the love that oozes from the heart of one so pure.*

Please know we watch over you, just as we do so many of you on the earth-plane, but those 'others' do not know this yet. (Obviously, as they read these pages they will). We can see the confusion that lingers and envelopes people in their lives and also upon their own pathways and existences which clouds their thinking. (Causing the illusion, we first spoke of.)

Their vision and senses are often blurred ... so they wonder and think, 'What on earth?' Or they may ask, "Please God, what do we do?" This can be related to all scenarios and in all circumstances for when there is trouble of the heart, the soul, or the mind David, you and every living thing turn to the one source and warmth and love who will listen to clarify each and every problem and situation.

For example, why does the parent who can't find their child or those in such despair then turn to God and ask for help? Do they ask for anything else? No, they do not. Is this clear, or are you still unsure about this and remain confused? Please do not be, for we will explain and therefore move and dissolve any pain.

Each individual(s) circumstance may be different but on the soul it is not and never will be. Also, at each experience or conflict the prayer and the call comes from 'within' and the cry is 'deafening'. Is this a sin? We know that whatever 'religion' you follow, whichever faith or belief, whatever nationality or the color of your skin, please know each living thing is connected. In every language you have all cried out in your deepest, darkest hour, "Please God, help me". (Even if you do not or have not believed 'He/she' could).

We ask you, 'Why would you say this, if deep inside you did not understand what you were asking for or where the help would come from? That question should now be quite clear. Perhaps it was in desperation or from pain deep within you? So, do you now understand the connection that pushes aside the clouds of the illusory deception?

On the other hand, you may have felt (or feel) help <u>can</u> arrive ... and also know within your heart God <u>can</u> do something about a certain predicament or pain. This is an immense understanding and clarification that goes way beyond the surface to the very core of each individual soul.

We hope that as you read this you do not become agitated or perplexed at this complex yet simple and real fact. Know strength is found when it is needed to be and in guidance too. So, as you pray for divine help know the cry is heard and the plea or scream, never absurd. This is because the creator is everything that is in each and every living fiber, tissue, energy flux, pulse, vibration, and frequency and is all the senses that every being possesses.

The creator ... all light, love, power, and energy are all around and holds out an open 'hand' to guide every single soul who wants to be 'found'. So, decisions that go way, way back in the individual's past lives 'history' are to be played out like a record 'track'. Perhaps to be repeated (if necessary) or released if truly desired and not held back.

What we would like to move on and say is that as each and every day goes by, we urge the individual to pause and reflect. One may *often cry, ponder and think of the light and of love but do not turn a blind eye. The divine source is to be clearly seen and is for you, for us and for 'all' to live and simply 'be'.*

Life is as complicated or as simple as you each make it and each of you can design or create it as you make it ... as you go along within your destiny. With this known, you can all struggle to come to terms with it or fly high like a beautiful, white dove. You could sing the words of love from a peaceful song, then move forward to help the crowd to reach out their arms to the 'ALL KNOWING ONE', who is both 'within' and above.

Know also that your own journey is to cope with the learning and the living process that you must complete. (For you have chosen these for your embodiment and its experiences to fulfill it). It is fighting the reality within you that can lead you to go off track, and therefore you will only see through that glazed and blurred wall of mist or glass. This needs smashing down with the love and light so that you can shatter the illusion to seek and move forward more clearly and to never ever look back.

We are now going to explain some information on your past-life regression and of what the many seeks to find and answer this way. Let us say we do not blame anyone for his or her curiosity or of the intrigue to look at the root of any problems you face this time around.

Indeed, many people have felt by going into the past has helped shape their futures, but this could also be said of many other avenues of course when you consider the history books of time and evolution, i.e., 'Learn by your mistakes' and the 'How else do you learn then?' etcetera.

However, we wish to say this is different and really does need pursuing. "Oh, but it's fun," some say. Or "To learn of my past and of what has happened to me would be helpful, as it could possibly happen again." Well, we do not wish to upset anyone but wish to now blow away some myths and push aside the illusion and confusion blocking an individual's progress.

First of all, you need to understand by concentrating only on the future (your time and perception not ours) can you progress? Only by changing the way you live, think, and feel for life and the way you love all things can true change take place. To live and debate on reality, a present-day reality and not what has passed 100, 1000, 10,000 years or more ago.

Secondly, each life and experience the individual (on a soul level) has passed through was for that period alone. What was learned then can only fully be deciphered and understood when another realm/plane of existence is reached.

We know the majority of those who conduct this research want to assist those who are desperately in need for release. They want to help them to live a clearer and more meaningful life. They also want 'proof' for themselves however and this leads us to say that if a 'regressions' therapist requires others to shed what they call proof then they need to ideally look for it themselves, within themselves!

This may sound critical. Please know we do not want it to come across this way, for we understand what has taken place has also been for reasons known by the creator ... to let the passing of certain knowledge 'flow'. Individuals will themselves have proof in their own hearts and minds (beyond any doubt), but the world and its masses will never be convinced on this type of evidence alone ... of re-incarnation, the soul's progress and of humankind(s) evolution. 100% proof to convince the human race this way will never, ever happen.

David, we know that a few years ago you actually undertook this technique and know 'all' of you there is to know. We saw your tears flow at the pain you went through and when you came 'around', your realization of the experience. Please could you add a few words to this passage to let others know of what we are trying to say because it is important that words also come from a source in your world and not just outside your (as some believe) imaginary screen or shell.

What I experienced was in a group (spiritual development) session, attended by 18-20 people and for me it really proved two things. First of all, I know it is true what the Trans-leátions have said, because I knew I had 'lived' before, this was confirmed by the overwhelming feeling of proof it had given to me ... and me alone. Afterwards, I described the regression [16] though I could not make other's believe in what I had shared with them. (How could I really make them understand the pain and loneliness I'd felt, as I died all alone in a cold, damp room, without a 'love' I could never have?

Secondly, what I have just said was obviously just a glimpse of my regression. You may start to feel and think, "I wonder if I could find out part of my own soul's history?" Or, "What good did it do him to live those emotions and pain ... through that particular lifetime's experience again?"

I would not be telling you the truth if I did not say that it fascinated me at the time. Yes, such curiosity, was it part of this journey and process? Also, I acknowledge the fact that although interesting, the pain relived and the tears that flowed from within me seemed to bring the hurt of that experience straight back to me. So, did (or does) this do me any good right now?

A past-life 'regression' therapist may say in reply, "But that is just one life, what about a happier one?" I think you have to judge for yourself and for your own personal growth, but I also feel you should also clear away the illusions to learn and live for today and not the past! Why? Well, would it actually enable you to pass this lifetime's tasks any easier or faster? Lastly on this, I have to say that because I've been fortunate to now 'grow' a little more in the love and light, perhaps this is why I now feel this way. (And I know you will too, either now or in the future.)

COMMUNICATION: *Thank you David for sharing your heart's information which we hope will be read and digested by many a nation. So then, finally on 'regression'. We feel you need to look forward into this life's 'future' to enable you to sustain and gain the progress that you and all of humankind both need. Answers will not be found to 'Ascend' to your new home that way. Not today, not tomorrow and never will.*

REGRESSION

To step back 'In' and 'To' your past lives known,
Is not the communication that will ever get you home.
You need to turn 'within' and find the love and light,
That will truly be your guide, each day, and every night.

By regression (and delving), into your soul's past life experiences,
Leads to confusion and interpretation ... of those many life appearances.
It shows the past that is revealed there, but will never shine anew,
For a living world that's gone, is not the future to now carry you.

We are also aware of those that are trying to find their future lives through future 'progression'. This both amazes and alarms us. Why? Well, if we were to state that we would not explain ourselves on this, some may think, 'It must be possible, but we are too frightened to say?

Let us point out that if you even knew of what was ahead (good or bad), do you think you could change it forever? Destiny cannot be! Can you prolong life or even shorten this life to get there? No, you cannot ..., for if you have not fulfilled what you are here to do and learn then you will choose what you need to live through again and again for it will be your choice on a soul level to do so!

Appreciate you have all yet to experience the one true connection of the creator's love and new home and you can only be called upon if the time is right and if it is right for you too.

Do not be misled or misguided by what others try to put into your head or your heart. You cannot live from the confusion but can truly live in peace and love and come forward to the everlasting source of 'life' itself. Never allow the illusion to take hold or throw you off balance for you are within arms reach of the divine light that can never be brought about by any tantalizing trance. So, please go forward and give your life a chance, for it will lead you to the glory and the loving light and forever in a merry dance.

Okay David, 'time' is drawing near and your energy fluxes are

From the Illusion ... and Confusion

changing ... you are still physically tired. We know you had earlier asked about some information regarding your animal kingdom on the earth-plane. Yes, we do know of the illness and decay and of the cattle's so-called 'disease' and you have asked the question, why? We have pondered on this; not because we do not know what to tell you (and all that read this), but because of the way we need to explain this to you. This will seem so harsh for people who love animals and know and understand what is a sacrifice.

Firstly, let us mention that it does not matter whether a single cow or eleven million cattle are killed / destroyed. Are these harsh and unkind words? From us, never! You know they will all be carried into the creator's light for they are part of you and they are part of 'me'.

Is the disease just a trick or a game? Or a justification for slaughter? Is it humankind's safe passage or for a digestive palate? Yes indeed, now think of the 'why', or the what for?

Time and time again animals have been the excuse for greed and to fulfill the need, but whose? The animals themselves (make no mistake) are not to blame as they were placed there and not from any shame. We will not want to condemn those in 'power' of legislation but they will know they will have to answer for their actions.

All we ask for is for those who care to pray from their hearts and what will be is their destiny. This is not to 'fob' you off or divert the question but to make you realize this (explanation) will be for all and their digestion. This book and the 'meat' are both pure from the heart and alive with love. It is what is around them that poisons and decays the inside or outer part. Is that a clue or a damning conclusion? It is for those who will know who must divert away from the confusion.

Do not hide from (or become hardened by) any pain that will be suffered. Instead, think of the light surrounding every living thing which suffers for we tell you nothing will 'die' for progress sake or is in vain. The answers, as we have said many times now, are within you all, so you must feel and understand this.

Well David, until the next time when the pen flows think of love and light and the beautiful peace and then project it all around you. Healing hands are so warm again as you have found out. You must also do this work, but of course ... there is no need to shout. Energy so strong is 'channelled' through and within to help those who feel ill and for their worries to be cast aside and also any sin.

Please, all of you lift up your hearts ... goodbye for now in love, truth, peace from us.

Thank you dear Father/Mother God, our creator and thank you also to the Trans-leátions and our many guides and teachers too. Bless you, all from my heart.

Monday 1st April 1996

Two days ago, I received a dream which at first was quite confusing, but I then understood I had been 'Astral Planning', which is not exactly a good way for learning or for spiritual growth. I thought to myself, was this an early April 'fool'… a spiritual joke? I knew I needed some further direction on this.

COMMUNICATION: *David, you must always raise your level of thinking and more importantly (over the last few days) you have again learned that from and to your heart's center is where the TRUE connection is made. It is there and there alone.*

Many lower 'planes' of consciousness and dimensions seek company and this is a distraction and their help arrives in other ways.

Again this is confusion and illusion not just for you, but all those who seek and are on their own 'pathway'. We feel that the dream and astral travel that you journeyed through to the particular 'plane' was something for you to experience and to learn from. (This was also meant to be). Therefore, do not feel you have let yourself (or us) down, but accept these learning steps and each process whereby you move forward and climb the 'rungs' of light.

We must also say that everything is (and has) its rightful place during one's spiritual growth. Progress can't be hurried ...

From the Illusion ... and Confusion

only through your acceptance and correct 'pathway' brings sustainable and worthwhile results.

Yesterday, you attended an 'Ascension Process' workshop [17] and we were also there together with many Ascended Masters [18] and guides too. (Remember, we all have a job to do in terms of love and light).

Much truth was spoken at this meeting and this has been digested on more subtle levels of energy and consciousness too.. You need to follow this true connection as it will help you to achieve what is in your destiny. Therefore, each new day provides you with the opportunity to learn what is required to overcome.

The inner conflict for enlightenment occurs across many planes of existence, and but they are too numerous to mention in great detail here. Yesterday the 3rd, 4th and 5th 'dimensions' were also described to you but again, we will not go into a full clarification of these as each individual must seek, learn and live with new (or old) information from 'other' sources at this moment of time.

It should be noted though that over the ages some knowledge has been misunderstood on these areas. So, please know that the 4th dimension does contain many souls and entities who are searching and travelling in 'lost' circles, and perhaps this is something they have to experience. Comprehend ... nothing is wrong in the overall plan set by the creator.

Those we refer to are always trying to grasp onto the light which emanates from within and around you. All you can do is to help them with your prayers and decrees [19] for their love and light to be returned. Do not think of them as bad or evil because they are part of the creation too, and the prayers sent will be their encouragement and direction, not their condemnation.

You must also raise and link to the 5th dimension for the progress that is

Required, and this can be achieved through meditation and prayer and by the constant turning 'within'–the linking of self to your Higher-Self [20]. This must always be so, for you all to learn and go on toward the infinite light.

Please also remember ... many teachers and guides are everywhere to help you. Their numbers are also infinite too because

Deliverance of Love, Light and Truth

they emanate from the only true source – the creator, the Great White Spirit, our Father/Mother God.

So, when uncertainty calls, ask for guidance and it will be given. Then, when you are ready to accept the test, you will accept it from the heart, your center of love and light. Sometimes this may all seem to be a struggle, but with the strength found there will come the belief and the love and the energy that is you and in every living thing.

Therefore, when difficulties envelop you and your life, do not think of or be dragged down to the lower self. Touch instead the feelings of your heart, your inner desires and wishes and simply connect with your Higher-Self from 'within' yourself. This way you will succeed and you will overcome all doubt and win. No, not a materialistic prize, but the reward of hope, love, and light so beautiful, so incomprehensible and yet so simple, real, and tangible to the inner senses as well as the so-called normal 'five' you utilize.

David, a thought has just flashed across your mind, 'What of those who have turned within but who maybe blind, deaf or dumb? Okay, even with any potential or actual physical disabilities they are also perfect because 'inside and out', you are born from the love of the purest light, that of the creator. From 'within' everything can be seen, touched, heard, tasted, smelt and known 'of' in so many more ways than each of those usual five, and therefore, all will learn and all will see the things the creator has set out for thee.

It is time to go now. The communication being short today, (just as you have requested) as your daily work is to be done. Please recall ... confusion does not begin inside but on those lower, outer vibrations. The illusions are now also required to be put aside to enable you to glow and shine and are not for you to hide.

Remember too, both information and wisdom are a release when the appropriate level of light is reached. Of this you will understand, because your teachers, guides and the Ascended Masters all go hand in hand.

Next time you <u>will</u> know it is us in your dream ... for two dreams cannot be the same, just as two flowers can never be. So, look for the Two Sisters symbol and then you will sense it is us and our name *alone. Hm, oh now you laugh, and we do too, 'E.T.', please phone home!*

Love to you all and in peace, truth and light please do trust. Goodbye for now from me and us.

Saturday 6th April 1996

My spirit guides, family and friends and the Trans-leátions, I need to communicate and receive your wisdom. You know what I have experienced in the last week and the profound effects these things have had on my heart, my mind and in my soul, in fact within my very 'being'. I do know that I AM THAT I AM, (God in me IS), but the confusion still continues, why?

Just when you think you are going in the right direction, the right pathway, you get knocked for six? A simple realization that what we know is but a minute speck of creation. And, in reality, there is so much more of the infinite source both inside of us and also of 'out there' too.

Someone has also said to me that channelling is wrong, and those who 'channel' are opening themselves to the lower planes and can be misled. Why do I pause and reflect upon such negativity? In fact, why am I even having these feelings at all when you have changed my life? Indeed, without you, I may not have been ready for a new or next step? Then there is the first book PATHWAY; which will surely help so many other people as well. Surely this can't be wrong, can it?

In addition, they stated, "The Ascended Masters have only decreed presentation to come through certain people who have previously ascended and who are now 'incarnate' again to help the earth-plane." There always seems to be this searching, yet coming up against illusion and confusion, or is it the truth?

You have also said there are as many paths as there are souls and you were given this task to help humankind through the creator. So, how can anyone judge this task and my task as insignificant and without purpose?

Can you also explain for us, is it true some Angels are Archangels who have fallen to the 4th dimension emit negativity energies?

Do they really try to lead us from reality? And if so, how can that be when they cannot speak the truth to us either collectively or as individuals? I am sorry to go on and on even though you did not wish to discuss these dimensions at this time but this seems all so relevant to me.

What should I do? Listen to within I know, but I ask these things and reach out to touch your heart for I know it is one of such love for us all.

Please can you guide us as there must be many people like myself who have come to this stage or point of growth. I very much wish to Ascend ... and understand this takes a lot of effort with prayer, meditation and decrees too, as well as the participation and guidance of the 'Masters' themselves. So help me please to clear the confusion that grasps and tries to hold me in a place that I long to break free ... to live in God's love, for eternity. Please come and talk and feel my love I send to you.

COMMUNICATION: *We are here again David, and we hear your hearts plea, to communicate through us and with us to thee.*

We have listened and heard your thoughts and of others too and of what has been said and will be done through you. Here is a word to describe your opening desires ... phew!

Okay, we are not, and never would be, amused at this, but what you seek and learn can be one of the same, or are they both in vain? Know we are not saying this just of you, but of the searching that goes on within (and out) and around people's hearts and minds.

First of all, go back to the earlier advice from our hearts, which are also connected to the true source of love and light, the creator. Do not judge one another for you are all individuals with your own search and pathway's too. The confusion still sets in because you open up to it during the searching and yearning. This is not wrong, but we reiterate this always reveals two sides or ideas. Lost or found, good or bad, glad, or sad ... two feelings and two thoughts. However, only if and when you find the one that fits you and your own needs will it click it into place. The truth must resonate inside you.

From the Illusion ... and Confusion

David, here are some important facts you already know but have only just (today) begun to relate to love and light.

Again we say we have never mentioned or decreed one evil thing to you or to those who will digest the 1st works (PATHWAY) or so on in the 'Deliverance'.

We are all connected, every fleck and every flux of energy. So, yes indeed, the 'I AM THAT I AM'.

Choices and goals. You seek and want to work towards your Ascension, but how do you really know whether anyone else has previously ascended? Have you read this, or is it because you feel it? Is it because someone else tells you so?

There is a time in everyone's hearts when the individual will know this, along with those who have achieved Ascension already with the creator know of it. Therefore, how can one say, "Yes, you are right, you have ascended?" Who can confirm it on the earth-plane in which you reside? Also, is it egotistic to say, "I have ascended" or "I am a master" (of this or that) to the masses who live and learn and who also desire to Ascend with you?

Before we go any further let us dispel something for those reading this and who might say, "That's strange, some of that last paragraph sounds as if it is quite negative, unkind or from the lower elements of the 4th dimension to me". We do not and never will say we know more than anyone of you ... or say that our advice is the only way either. Therefore, those who seek and learn of the cosmic map or 'plan', try to decipher it as best as you can.

Hopefully, you can ascertain what we say to you is only to help and assist you. Not a rule (book) or law or set of commandments. Try to grow not from the mind, but from the heart's center for <u>all</u> wisdom and knowledge is implanted there. No deception, no false creativity or deviation of any kind is there to trick, slow down or blow you off course or away.

The connections to the information in the first book continue as a guide to you all and we do not sit on a golden chair to convey, 'Thou shall or thou shall not, or else!' We do not live this way or sustain ourselves from the creator's source of love and light any other way other than to nurture all who have turned to their hearts listen to the creator. (As do all who work within the creator's ambiance and most powerful light energy.)

So you see, the course you take is fine but only as long as it leads to progress for yourself. If you can help others along their path then of course this is fine to. No one should mislead another, and we can say there is none from us. Please ask yourself, how could that ever be the case when we are connected to Heaven's cords of love and light ... just as you are. Does that make anyone better than you or us? No, for we are all equal in the love and light ... and when you live in its peace, you live to learn not to fight.

The inner explorations you each come across form part of your growth and without it you would be forever (?) lost. Therefore, you can discuss between each and all of you on what has been said. You can also read, meditate, pray and pray again. Are these or anything associated with them 'bad' in any way?

You will never, ever, ever stop learning as we have said before! Living and learning in the light is infinite. Remember this, and you will ascend with both the physical 'presence' and the soul ('I AM') Christ presence, the 'God' in me 'IS'. Do you understand David?

Yes I do. (The energy and heat around my physical body was incredible at this point!)

COMMUNICATION: *We are glad. You must now go from strength to strength and remember that we are always here for you. Also know that no matter what frequency level you attain (and you will fulfill your destiny) you will forever be part of us. So, my son, it does not matter what route you take or follow to achieve your goal. Just live in peace and trust for it will surely flow.*

To reiterate, we understand others might state, "Channelling is wrong, for it can cause confusion, and that it's dangerous/ evil" and of course we accept this viewpoint as being an individual's choice, and you must too. However, you know inside your heart, how much does it really matter what other people think or feel of this?

Tell me, when Jesus was on the earth-plane and was chastised and persecuted, did he ever stop to think, 'I will not continue on my

From the Illusion ... and Confusion

path of love and light because others may think...' Think what? That he was evil or that he misled people? Did it matter?

Does it matter even now? He touched millions and millions of hearts and souls and of course, he still does, despite everything He suffered. So, how relevant is it when you have accepted and know that, 'I AM THAT I AM', the Christ consciousness, the Higher-Self is with you ... within you, and all around you forever?

Follow your heart. Look beyond the stars and along Heaven's pathway and door and embark upon your true goal to save and love your soul. By doing so, you will find that all this information inside your heart is the truth, because as we have said earlier, it is connected to the creator this way.

Exterior forces (both negative and positive) will influence and guide you, and these are what you will need to decide upon for yourself. Whether they will help you complete the tasks or if you need them at all will be down to you. Remember, Jesus (as the prime example of God's love) needed no 'prop's or magical potions and used no force, no pressure to progress and you do not either. The outcome reflects your choices which are constructed from your own desires and character and personality. We do not say you cannot use these attributes, but only ask whether you need any of them at all. Inside the stillness and true peace, your perceived identity formed by your memories disappears. Ultimately, only you can answer the question concerned.

Also, as your friend recently stated, has it really taken two thousand years for the 'penny' to drop? I.E. For those who wish to take up and acknowledge the barriers around their soul to make their ascension ... their 'goal'? What we mean here is that each of you will have learned what you need to learn whether this information is way beyond BC or not.

You now have a choice, to continue the treadmill of 'death and rebirth' or embark the everlasting life in 'light'. This is a special opportunity and we urge you all to take it. We will not elaborate on the 'why?' because you can determine this for yourselves. Maybe you could take another look at chapter one of Pathway – 'Love and Life, or Destruction' and try and feel the images inside you, which may help you to make your own decision.

Deliverance of Love, Light and Truth

David, we would like to tell you we understand the confusion and the searching that you and many others are now going through. This is natural due to the current chaos that exists upon the world in contrast to the cords of light piercing through the twisted darkness.

Vibrations of light are expanding, but the planet you live upon is too and it is the combination of such which have an effect on each and every one of you. Again, this is part of your destiny at this time to work through to your goal that has been set by yourselves and from the creator's love and light.

So, from these communications, you will learn and also grow too. However, it is what you all do with that growth that is important, for we are also all part of the creator's 'love'. Therefore, it will be for others on the earth-plane to decide whether we do, or do not 'fit'. It is not our desire to say we are here or there or above or below in the course of things, for this too is for people to make their own conclusion. Whether they feel it is important to do either of these things it does not matter, because we know of our task and our goal, and so we ask, 'Is it now time to find yours?'

Please know we have not been forced or instructed to help only one particular planet and civilization, or certain beings or souls and not others who may be here or there or wherever you may think of throughout the universe.

We have been honored beyond comprehension to leave these messages across the Universal spectrum of light in millions of galaxies. So, please know that humankind is only one part of the overall 'plan' of light ... but are also special and unique too. In addition, the source of learning you now have embarked upon is not wrong. So ... judge for yourselves, are we?

David, it is time to go now and time for you to relax too. Chapter One, although already quite long is almost complete. For now, through your experiences beyond the boundaries of the senses you will reach attainment ... though new initiations and prayers and through the release of your self to your Higher-Self. Yes, the Christ presence and consciousness, the 'I AM THAT I AM' will become 'one' forever! Bless you, all. May love and light be forever in your hearts and minds ... and eradicate the 'ego', disruption, hate or darkness, and only the creator can you then but 'find'. Love to you all and peace and trust within. For now, goodbye.

May the love that flows from my heart always reach you. Thank you for hearing my call today ... I needed your strength, wisdom and light so much. David.

Monday 15th April 1996

Dear, dear Trans-leátions, it seems so long ago (yet only nine days have passed) since the 'pen' last flowed.
There are things I need to ask you. I hope for new learning to progress and seek your advice and assistance, so I can pass on your wisdom for others to grow too. Will today be the last part of chapter one, the 'Illusion and Confusion'? Please link and help me as I may have missed your dream signals. It just seems so long ago, please come through my consciousness.

COMMUNICATION: *Dear, dear David. We are here and of course we hear your call, your request, your plea and understand your needs and of others too.*
We have deliberated and waited for you to connect the 'pen' with us. We wanted to give you some breathing space to think and to sort things out in your mind and your heart. We know this feels the same way for many of you on the earth-plane ...every morning, noon and night and many have the desire to take flight on new ways of thinking and of feeling.
Each of you desires to strive and thrive on fresh bits of information. Some are easier and some more difficult to understand than others but nonetheless, they all serve a purpose in the overall plan of life. We also see you are trying new prayers, meditations, and decrees. This is good because it will clear some of what is holding you back, and we will explain this further in due course.
As you have all been informed of karma and destiny in many ways of learning like books, lectures and information from different pathways and roads, we now wish to open your hearts and minds to new thinking. Your soul journey enables you to erase karmic debt

Deliverance of Love, Light and Truth

from your true being and become raised to a higher vibration level.

Having been instructed of your imbalance and the tasks to overcome this, (on an inner level), it is time to over-ride what has held so many back on the treadmill of death and rebirth. Please know you all have the opportunity to succeed if you feel you have the need! The choices are always yours ... the individuals alone. No force, no coercion, no push or pull or any twisting of your hand or hearts or minds.

The illusion and confusion of this destiny is the belief that others can do it for you, but no person is able to do that. You can be advised and assisted with information (as we said earlier), but it is you who has to take control of the self and combine with your 'Higher-Self' to proceed down the right pathway of love, light and truth. The royal road provides the only choice, for there lies the power of the creator itself and all the Heavenly 'bodies' both imaginable and also incomprehensible.

So, if you correctly tap into this you will need not further guidance because that source is 'all knowing', 'all giving' and 'all loving'. We, like many others, are just a relay, a circuit or a connection to the goal, an assistant if you like. However, we cannot change anything you do or do not possess within the inner you.

Any change or adjustment or remission of karmic laws/destiny can only be granted from the creator itself in the connections that are with your self and your Christ consciousness. Therefore, this can only be done by cleansing and clearing the bodies you possess and realign your cord of light that emanates infinitely in length from the 'I AM THAT I AM' presence within you to the creator itself.

We have heard many of you say your auras are this big and so wide, or they radiate here and there. However, know that your cord of light from your 'self' will remain invisible to even those who 'see' these things on the earth-plane ... and your science or technology will not be able to picture or photograph it.

Let us retrace our steps for a moment. We have just said that no one else can assist the outer 'you', except for guidance and direction only. As such, the real task is yours and this will remain true for all. Conversely, when you have turned within and realized

From the Illusion ... and Confusion

what needs to be done for your progress, you will then receive the further help you need each minute, day and year. This continues until you, as individuals are ready to ascend and have cleared all the necessary karma you possess on a soul level. You would have also passed initiations and followed steps laid down by the creator through the love and light 'hierarchy' to fulfill the connection.

We know of the Summit Lighthouse/University *[21]* where some of your recent 'thinking' has come from David and this will help you and the many as we have said before. There is much truth in what has been said and learned from these sources and expanded out from who received them. The prayers, decrees and songs will lift people's hearts and clear karma this is true, but always remember it is you who makes it happen ... through your thoughts words and deeds.

Like many other things in humankind's history, the belief and the strength of their conviction has carried the many or often just a few, but this strength alone will not be enough. You must do and say and feel these things with the very love and light deep inside. Too many people talk and act without emotion and expect they're being cleansed 'within', yet all they are doing is temporarily clearing the mind and nothing else.

How can anyone really progress if their strength is not from their heart? Or if their conviction does not materialize from deep inside themselves and their inner 'self'? Lip service toward many things are the words that flashed across your mind David, and they can be used quite appropriately here, can they not? So, with that said, now let us get off this slightly negative track to let the light of understanding flow in the only true direction, from your hearts.

Your karma, built over many of your 'lives' and through countless experiences has come to a point where your soul is saying, "Have I had enough of this?" (This of course is in basic terms). Do you also remember when we asked in book one—Pathway, to try to picture the strongest love and peace you could ever imagine and multiply it by infinity? Now ask yourself, would you not want to experience and stay within Gods love and to return to your true home?

Of course! So, it is the time to lift up your hearts to the universal

Deliverance of Love, Light and Truth

light source ... and connect from your centre with the ability to travel the cord within your very being and soul! Could this be today, tomorrow, this year or next year? Each of you on a soul level through the creator and the creator's light hierarchy knows the answer to that question. Just try to progress as much as you can in peace and love and above all, trust.

Please also know your karma you hold resembles sticky molasses surrounding your heart's flame. In simple terms, when the darkness has been erased and replaced with pure light then you will be ready to embark on your journey and ascend to your new 'home'. The only way to proceed is to purify your heart's flame through your actions, thoughts and emotions. This is also done with continual connection to your Higher-Self/Christ consciousness through prayer, meditation and decrees from the heart, mind and soul.

You remove past karma each day that has been set for you when you live this way and when the process is maintained you can clear your karma from yesterday, last week, last year and back to many previous lifetimes. You can also clear and move forward through each coming day, week, month, and year and so on. Please note this is not an easy thing to do in the sense that, "Oh, I have prayed today, so I am okay". It has to be much more than this and with sincerity and passion and belief through thoughts of love. They must form part of your busy, busy lives.

Individually, you must seek what direction to take and where and what information to take on board and learn. We are not here to say that a particular prayer, for instance, will save you. If that sounds strange you might want to put this book down right now. God, the Great Spirit (or whatever name you feel comfortable with) is in you and IS you. This is why the savior is yourself ... because you are part of the creator.

The illusion and confusion regarding your destiny is mapped out through the truth of you. However, it can only be altered and changed in one way, and that's by turning within to connection of the self as we keep reiterating.

So, your karmic slate <u>you</u> yourself have accumulated and written. It does not have an ending, as there isn't one ... you can only rewrite

From the Illusion ... and Confusion

the next chapter; your next page or 'day' of your life for it is all down to you. This is what we are trying to explain ... that you have the ability to change yourselves and your way of life and world and this is why the opportunity is so special. Please take it. You can make this 2nd, 3rd or 4th and final wave of ascension but it will eventually be you who can only decide to embark upon this journey.

We wish you success and truth always and in love and light we bless. Turn away from darkness and confusion then the light will shatter all illusions. Every cell and molecule and energy vibration and particle that is misshapen within you and around you will disappear.

Well, David, it is time for us to go now. Bless you, for this pen flowed. Chapter Two is now due and this will be called 'FOREVER TO BE TRUE'. It will be diverse and contain many subsections of information and clarification for you all. Before then, we will meet you in a dream and you will then know when it is to start. Goodbye for now. We love you all.

Thank you from my heart and may God bless you all too.

CHAPTER TWO: 'FOREVER TO BE TRUE'

Saturday 27th April 1996

Dear Trans-leátions, it is now twelve days since we have last communicated though it seems so very much longer. Each night I have waited for your signal and dream message, yet somehow I sense that you know how I feel today and this is why I need to connect with you.

I feel ill, physically sick and my mind is constantly pounding with vibrational energy/pressure as if to tell me, 'You are not listening' or perhaps it is a sign to say, 'Hey, we are here and waiting?' Have I missed a dream or a message (again?), or has your signal been blocked? If so, why, who or what would do this? Maybe it is myself?

All I know is that my heart wishes to feel your love and your wisdom to help me and carry me along. If this is wrong for me today, then all I can say to whoever is listening or watching over me, I am sorry. I am also perplexed at a letter that arrived for me this morning. A publisher has declined 'Pathway'. It seems that someone has a closed heart (not wrong, for that is their choice), or perhaps those who make these decisions are not ready for their hearts to be prized open at this time?

Please come MILLANDERER [22], please come Trans-leátions and hear my plea from my heart this day, for I know that we will never part. As I now 'open' to you, (a part of the creator's love and light), there is the truth I cannot deny, that we are all one ... connected forever by the love of the divine! Please come and let this pen flow. Please show us part of the wonderful light and love of the universal light source.

COMMUNICATION: *My son, my dear, dear son, we are here and we are going to bring you cheer ... make no mistake of that.*

Deliverance of Love, Light and Truth

(Suddenly ... a flash of intense brilliant light seemed to flow through my body and my mind. Somehow I could see, feel and sense 'within' this beautiful being of light. (PICTURE THREE: WELCOME).

COMMUNICATION: *Yes my son, our hearts are open to hear your plea and your many needs. Our arms will engulf you wide, and we acknowledge your flow of feelings from a hearts rough ride.*

We had not sent you a dream David and you have not misread any of the dreams that have entered your mind or awakened those thoughts deep inside your heart. We have been waiting for your earthly time to pass ... for those days and nights and challenges to come through, so that you can forge ahead on your one true love and lights pathway ... your destiny.

Remember, each obstacle people overcome is for the purpose of individual growth and learning. So, both the so-called ups and downs in your life(s) together may be experienced as karma [23]. However, you need to live and shed the imbalance during today, tomorrow, and so on until you are cleansed sufficiently to Ascend as we have said before.

So, has today become another test? The letter you received is not what we had expected either. This proves that no matter what we know and can do in the light that we do not know everything ... though we have never implied we do, have we? Only the creator itself can decree such things, and we are all part of the complex and yet simple overall plan.

PICTURE THREE: 'WELCOME'

We have thought and come to our own conclusions on this peculiar event and as you say, perhaps closed hearts and minds? Negativity and darkness try to slow down the increasing vibration levels wherever it can but has it succeeded? No! It is merely a short delay (in a sense) of what is inevitable.

The book 'Pathway' is to be directed to a different location. Understand that it will be published because it is part of us and part of the 'all knowing' love and light. When something contains so much love it cannot be denied, because truth will shine even brighter to overcome anything. This current obstacle of structured

Deliverance of Love, Light and Truth

viewpoints will be moved aside. Not with or by a punch or kick, but with a gentle loving hand or kiss.

This of course is not 'physical', but a connection to someone else ... their heart and thoughts will knock them for six, 'bowled over' you could well say. Therefore, do not feel downhearted, because this is just a delay and not really significant. It is merely a brush with frustration where your physical resides.

David, we watch over you and we now close in around you as your pen flows. (Though of course you do not see us with your sight). So, close your eyes for a moment and sense us with your heart. Maybe then you could draw what you feel as it may help inspire someone else's heart too.

The candle flame suddenly increased to over 8-10 inches (ca. -25 cm) high whilst time seemed to simply drift and fade away. I felt I was being lifted, as if being raised up into a craft. You (the Transleátions) were there. A few of you were in a circle. I saw in the center you were building something, not a material apparatus, but of the mind. Your thoughts were 'manifesting' and my consciousness had become part of you to 'see'.

A brilliant light began to shine above the earth and a bridge of some kind began to be constructed. It seemed so strange and yet ... it was not. At the base of this bridge, books and 'works' of history formed the steps and its support, as if they were the foundations, the building blocks to help all humankind. My heart, my very being skipped a beat for 'PATHWAY' was there side by side with the Bible, the Quran and the written 'word' of many religious 'leaders' from many planes of consciousness and vibration levels/energy.

Deliverance of Love, Light and Truth also began to form and create a new step upon this bridge of 'light'. Then, the steps above these were being paved with something else. I recognized lots of books, which were opened in the middle to reveal pictures of a heart. I knew instantly this was to symbolize that we 'cross' and climb to the creator with what is here and all around us, but most importantly, we 'cross over' only with an open-heart.

I also knew that the symbolic picture of a heart meant that you always only have to turn to your heart's center, for it is there that the foundations will support and carry you forever in (and to) the love and light. (PICTURE FOUR: 'THE BRIDGE TO AN OPEN HEART').

This scene began to fade so I gazed to one side. There on the right, Millanderer stood by some sort of window or screen. I could see beyond him into deep space. A most beautiful light starts getting brighter and brighter with rays of 'light' shining and emanating in all directions from it. Again, I knew this was the creator's <u>new</u> home (a plane of consciousness and vibration) that was coming together for all 'beings' to share.

Spheres of light were also connecting and spiraling, sparkling brilliantly like diamonds. I know such peace will be for all eternity in the creator's true love that is and does contain everything. Suddenly my 'mind' ... my consciousness fades and you (the Trans-leátions) seemed to disappear from my view, yet I also know remain here with me.

COMMUNICATION: *My son, you have seen and felt with nothing else but an open-heart and mind, and now the picture you have drawn will help others of your own kind. So, you see, what had happened with Pathway was but a small distraction and maybe try to throw you—or us—off guard. Now you can make up your own mind over such thing.. Send the book in another direction from your heart and then the joy and the raising of your arm in triumph will be felt so high and so far. A victory in a personal sense and yes, such joy will be heaven sent.*

Love and light that is true will always succeed and though tough times may make the heart bleed with emotions and frustrations, but you can and will overcome them. Did Jesus not lead the way once before ... and are you now all realizing the score?

There are many, many scriptures and there is much truth throughout different cultures and time spans of history not only on your earth, but in millions of other worlds too. Perhaps all of those have said, "But I just do not know what to do" or, "I haven't got a clue!" Then, with realization they turn within and find their true selves and their true goal. To ride upon the cord of light and to draw open the final curtain. To raise their souls high as a beacon ... or a signal from a ship's mast like a flag upon a pole. A simple communication to both the individual and the masses to raise their hearts and vibration levels to become 'one' ... the light eternal and grow away from the closing structure of both the mind and of being just 'man'.

David, you are never, ever alone and all you need to do is to call to the love and light whether it is your day or in the depths of you night. We will hear you and those that need or wish to will too. Also know the hierarchy of God's creation are there for you, in fact, Angels and Archangels are with you all. They will direct your route and protect you as well, and many light-bearers will also grow and can go on to 'tell'.

So, all the teachers of God's love and truth (who reside in 'His' name) await the individual call from your individual heart's flame. The three-fold flame of your true heart is burning bright and the 'blooms' of this (of your soul's flame) will cry out in the truth of love and light's name.

PICTURE FOUR: 'THE BRIDGE TO AN OPEN HEART'

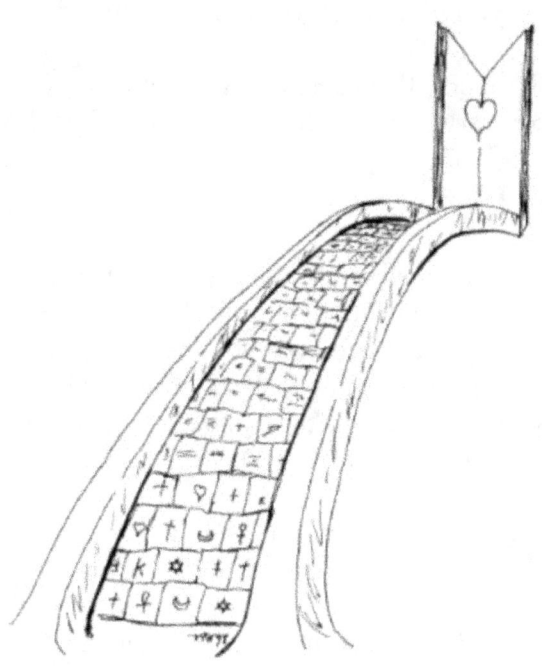

It is now 'time' for us to go my son, but you will get the dream message when the time is right for the pen to flow again. Trust your instincts and intuition and then return Pathway out into the light ... to beat on the door of a true soul's heart and their true soul's flame. It will be published in one or the other and all the work will never be in vain.

Deliverance of Love, Light and Truth

We love you and love you all and always will. Grow in strength ... even from a backward step. Then take two forward steps upon the bridge of light this night, and then you will win and you will be all right.

To you all, may love and light be received from each and every plane of love through the power of God, the creator of everything. We wish you well and want you to all succeed. Open your hearts this day and feel the truth bursting out to sustain your real need, the one and only true 'feed'. Bless you all ... and goodbye from our hearts.

I love you so much. Please know that the peace and love from this pen is so overwhelming. It is so beautiful. Thank you.

Friday 17th May 1996

During last night I experienced a 'visitation'. I seemed to have been awakened from a deep sleep to find two 'gray' figures in the bedroom. One appeared at the end of the bed and the other one to my side. As they moved nearer to me, I did not feel any fear and was more surprised than anything else. As they moved closer, a question came into my mind, 'Are you ready now David?' I believed I was, but for what?

Suddenly a brilliant white light emanated and shone around the room, bursting like fragments of shard glass from behind and through the curtain in the bedroom window. I glanced at the digital alarm clock; it's neon red numbers lit up at 02.06 am. Then there was an immense rushing; pulsing sensation and I felt I was zooming to and from a magnificent 'Star' of light ... to become part of this light.

Then, as if piercing through an explosion of color, 'I' came to rest at the base of some steps upon a bridge. It was as if I had been sucked upward at tremendous speed and straight through the front cover of Pathway! Such an amazing peace and feeling of love enveloped me with an understanding and realization, which came to my heart with these words, "THIS IS YOUR PATH AND YOUR LIFE".

It seemed that as quickly as this all began, everything then started to fade. It was as if I was just drifting, then slowly sinking back into my bed to fall asleep.

(Again?) I awoke, and looked over at the clock. It read 6.00 am and I immediately (and instinctively) knew some sort of step forward or leap in my perception or understanding had taken place inside of me. I also felt extremely privileged too.

Straight away I wanted to analyze what had happened to me. Perhaps in a rational way, or to think of some so called 'normal' explanation for this event. This could have been, (and some would say it was) Hypnopompic Imagery [24], or maybe Temporal Lobe Liability [25]?

Thursday 23rd May 1996 (11.00 am)

After saying a few prayers, I became 'still', and I heard (clairaudiently) a voice saying to me, "Here is what you must do to succeed and make everything come true".

A FRIEND'S MESSAGE

Be you and be yourself in all that's said and done,
Be good, by connecting to the all-loving 'One'.
These 'times' are most difficult, and they try their best to undo,
All the hard work you and others ... have been through and through.

So listen, please listen to your heart and to your soul,
Then go on to fulfill your only one true goal.
And pray and then be 'still', as much as you all can,
For the pen will always flow, receiving light from other land's.

So much to be learned, and soothing like a song,
And yes, you're right my son, we are ready to go on.
For we've all watched and seen, of what's been happening,
So never feel alone ... if what's said is loud or deafening.

No ... it is all 'inside, so turn within as you know how,
And we give you this new message, as it's for the here and now.
Yes, David we're your friends, and of a true star family,

Deliverance of Love, Light and Truth

Though you did not expect this, or had you almost finally?

You've waited for so long, and that was always of the 'plan',
But now it's truly over, you'll grow to fulfill this new 'time span'.
So be ready and both willing, and please set the time aside,
For we're forever always with you, and we will never, ever hide.

My son when you next sit, and feel you are alone,
Be prepared to grow and learn, and let it flow until your 'Home'.
Love and wisdom and the truth, is all around in every place,
And we promise to light the world ... and put a smile upon your face,

But for now, it is goodbye ... until you progress and then move forward,
My son we always love you, and will never lead you wayward.
We'll speak soon to lift your heart, so end finally with this 'note',
We simply love you all, and wish to keep your soul and mind afloat.

Thank you for your love and peace and truth. I had missed you all so much.

Tuesday 18th June 1996

It's been almost four weeks since our last 'full' communication, and it really does seem awfully long ago. Please, hear me dear Transleátions. Help me grow and know and enable what is given through this 'pen' to become a way forward for those of love and truth. I thank you again for your poem yesterday. I've missed you and have waited. Bless you always and may your love shine though, forever.

COMMUNICATION: *My son, we are here and are connected as always, as 'one'.*
David, please describe the feeling you have just experienced.

Phew! Such pressure is all around me, a pulsating energy that feels as if am encompassed by a layer of something really light and gentle. It's like I am being wrapped in a shawl of silk, so pure and soft to touch. At this precise moment there is such immense warmth which envelopes me and I thank you so much for this peace and tranquility.

COMMUNICATION: *Yes, we have come to you David, both to be with you and to become still in our oneness. Know we have never left you and never will, no matter how easy or difficult it is to climb or overcome the 'hill'.*

Many 'paths' are crooked or bent and many of you still sit on the fence. But, if you try to clear the screen you'll read and digest what is said and then understand what we mean.

Time and time again we see the puzzling expressions of the many and the feeling of doubt over which way to go. We say go with the flow ... simply go with the flow. Use your intuition for it will guide you and the end result ... your inner and outer goal will come to fruition.

Today, we will talk mostly in rhyme and reason, perhaps a communication for each of you to help you through the seasons. (David, a thought flashed through your mind of autumn, winter, spring and summer. It could mean this but clear the mind of your earth-plane thoughts.) Your seasons and years can be good or bad and full of joy or sad. Or if they have been so immersed in pain, then may the cool of the rain or warmth of the 'Sun' now guide and lead you to the everlasting one!

The 'season' we speak of is life with its ever-changing path and track, so please learn your own way of truth to never look back. It is for you to understand your free will and discover the future. Whether it has been written within 'stone' or if your life and your heart can turn to the light to find your true home.

Similarly, the glory and beauty beyond your comprehension exists within parallels of 'time' and space. Yet we say today, you are staring at it all and it is right in front of your face! You could rightly ask, "Where? For I do not see, has something blocked my eyes or heart with a sheet of darkness? Or, "Why does it never happen to me?" Shh, shh, dear child of the light. All in time, just live your life right.

Deliverance of Love, Light and Truth

Every day you are given an opportunity to shine and cast off your doubts and kick off the sublime. Yes you are busy and though we understand this and know of your needs to eat, sleep and look after yourself and family (which will always be high on your daily list); but does this mean that you will probably miss? We will explain this.

It is easy to divide time for one purpose or another for my family, my home, my job, and everything I normally do will always come first. However, please look at that statement more carefully. Everything is connected and never divided. So the light was, is and always shall be.

Now take your thoughts back to today's events and before you read this page of this book. Could you have touched, helped, asked, said, given your words or expressed yourself in any other way? A way of light, a way that would have changed even the smallest part of your life or of those around you to make a more loving and a more 'happier' environment?

You see, everything you say and do or feel and everything that is part of your daily lives is in fact fragments of your karma and karmic imbalance. Is this absurd or preposterous? It may sound like this if you ask, "How can such things have an impact on myself or upon others? Why do I have to be so true"?

Try to go beyond normal reasoning of cause and effect and of action and reaction. Nothing is complicated. Nothing is confusing. Just know and understand that love and light 'IS' (and is from) the creator.

TO OPEN ... AND EXPLORE

The words that you speak, the tone of your voice and the touch of your hand,
Contains the energy from creation ... to each and every land.
But do these thoughts now come 'within' ... or only through your brain,
And if they race off track, will you feel it's all in vain?

Both your love and your anger, can be deemed one of same,

Forever To Be True

Though are they divided by ... an imaginary line or bleeding vein?
So every action and your deeds ... flow from endless 'nought',
Lies the choice to live forever, separated by 'planes' you've always sought.
Yes a magical number, that exists from your hearts center,
Both returns and forever spirals, on to the never, never.

It's so simple to understand, just brighten your 'self' right to the core,
To start to really know, the 'one' and only score.
That you are beautiful light, the source and frequency of love,
In everything and all directions ... so don't believe it's just above.

We know that some people may still be confused by what we say. Therefore, we have given you a picture that will touch you 'inside' and ask you to no longer hide. Try to be 'still' within, so we can connect with thee, your consciousness and physical too. David, an image will now come through, be strong so you may feel it too. (PICTURE FIVE: THE FOUR)

This picture of the 'Cross' could signify a religion to many but may be unrecognized or refuted by others. Please broaden your thinking (is all we ask), for the spectrum of colors running through the cross represent many things. Perhaps more to those who 'see' the truth inside themselves, and less to others who have yet to discover their true purpose and goal. Let us explain further.

The creator's light contains everything and is within each and every frequency and color and every source of life. Indeed, the 'spectrum' represents initiations of progress within the planes of existence and those of your life too.

The four directions can represent your North, South, East, and West or the four winds which scatter the seeds of love ... or do you think they cause unrest? The four points represent your life cycle too, and the number of times that humanity has evolved to this level of progress before. It also signifies your 'bodies': Mental, Physical, Emotional and your Astral/Etheric 'self'.

What you (the individual) need to consider is what all this means to you. Therefore, know you are all part of evolution and the creator's loving and flowing 'Tree of Life'. Each person will feel

Deliverance of Love, Light and Truth

something different but this does not matter, as long as they can move away from darkness and hate and from the misleading statements of other people.

In your heart you will sense what is right for you. That special 'something' may not be for anyone else on the whole of your planet or in fact, upon any other 'plane' or level of existence. As long as you feel and live and learn with love and light it is irrelevant. "Do what you feel and feel what you do and all your dreams will come true." A statement [26] you recently heard from Jesus, did you not my son?

So, you see, going back to what we explained earlier ... everything you see, feel, think, and do resonates positive and negative energy. It can lead to truth, love and light or cause pain, anguish and make you (or others) feel down or sad. Therefore, we ask for you to open up and pray so that peace and love can rain 'in' and shine across the world.

PICTURE FIVE: 'THE FOUR'

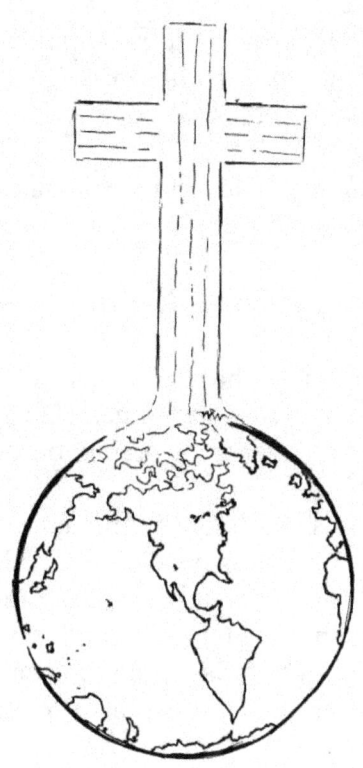

Please appreciate your destiny is in your own hands. A heavy burden is not what we wish to place upon you but just wish to express our love for all-living things and light energy ... and for you to be true.

David, it is time to go now my son and we are so glad you understand what took place on the 17th of May. You did not realize it at first, but we were in your bedroom ... to feel your love and wipe away your tears. You will never fear, not while we are with you.

Comprehend you are all different, so beautiful and part of the creator's plan of love and life. You are the energy of 'light' itself. Love, feel, and accept it for you are 'it'. Start to live and change and raise every structure in your being, so you can go beyond the barriers of the physical and the senses ... to remain in peace and bliss forever.

'Till the pen flows once again, love to you all. In peace and love do trust.

Thank you from my heart. I love you and will always be here for you.

Saturday 1st June 1996 (2.45 pm)

Dear Trans-leátions, such a busy week has just passed. Please help us to expand and not to divide our time. Help us to understand that we do not need to place constraints on ourselves or upon those around us.

I would like to ask for more information on the structure of this book, is this okay? Will the titles of each chapter follow on after each one is completed, (as in Pathway), or can you reveal them all now? For some reason I feel this is important.

As I write these few words I feel such warmth enveloping me and I know that you are here. Please let this flow through me, and for my love and heart to be open to truth, peace, and light forever. I feel so privileged and immensely proud.

COMMUNICATION: *My son, no massive bursts of energy, but a simple tug of your heart to realize we are here. We will never part from you or from anyone who has love in their soul.*

We have gathered here today, this hour and this minute of your time and space to connect together and wish to relate further information for you to take on board. However, there is no pressure to move too quickly, because your perception can become strained or occasionally weak.

Even after many explanations, it can still be difficult for someone to accept and declare they can follow their own truth. We have often seen how a huge change of mindset (and knowledge) can confuse or increase an already fragile state of mind, which prevents the continued search for both the individual and the masses. This can occur because even though there is a need to move forward in wisdom and general spiritual education within their hearts flame, (as the Ascension process gathers pace), one must accept and comprehend each step taken upon the enlightenment trial.

Confusion can lead those who have just started to 'open' (like a beautiful flower bud warming to the summer Sun), to close once again before the darkness of the night. It is as if something evil, (like a mysterious heavy blanket), has been placed over it, weighing it down, forcing a struggle within once more. So, will the light both raise or be seen again?

The reader of these works or books can follow each part like the links of a chain ... made of love. Or, perhaps, they could sense a guiding white light which shines brightly through the gaps of an imaginary wire mesh ... which has continually trapped those to live life in a darkened tangled mess. Perhaps a certain picture, poem, page, or chapter can lead them to the answer they seek.

A truth or guided words may apply to an individual or even as a collective. Everyone will be different, yet each will be the same. How can that be and what do we mean? Well, you are all unique, with separate abilities and characteristics and this is why you believe you are diverse, when all along you are 'one' of the light and love of the creator. Nothing but God can erase that or change this fact. However, we can now hear a question that may be fired straight back, "Well, prove it then!"

What would you like us to do? Perhaps we could scream or shout or descend upon you with great power and force of a so-called 'Godly' act? We laugh, a wry smile across each 'face', for time and time again, a similar reaction occurs across many galaxies and across multiple time frames and space.

The learning process (or acceptance) can be instantaneous or

Deliverance of Love, Light and Truth

like some, taking millions of years. Nonetheless, in due course, everything will overcome all doubts and fears. Nothing will be given with an iron fist or hand, but with (and from) a guiding light from within oneself, and from many light bearers from numerous planets, as well as other planes of existence and lands too.

The guidance and wisdom you all seek comes from inside you, through one's faith, trust and the love that must be firstly understood. As mentioned before, you cannot progress if you pay 'lip service' to the truth within you. (This is not intended to be a deriding statement to upset or hurt you.) As we have just said, to withdraw from living a life of joy and peace will resemble a blanket placed over a light, blinding it in artificial darkness which can only diminish the growth of the seed of life. That said, you could only do what you do within your own capabilities.

David, we read your thoughts and feelings. You, like many, would like to wave a magic wand to change the earth in an instant. And many wish to create peace and love and to feed the planet's starving millions, or clothe the cold and guide the strong to help the weak ... yes, to unify the light in a second, a minute, a day or a week?

We reiterate you can only do what you can. How far one can affect others for good is not only down to the individual, but also the exterior forces and energies which lie all around and guide or prevent an event, a decision, or life changing action to commence and fulfill itself.

By linking together with hands of love you can accomplish so much more. However, remember those two statements, those two opposites that highlight the tasks ahead. Perhaps one could say, "What's the use ... I might as well give up!" or,

on the other hand, "Yes, I will gain strength in my conviction to live and learn and teach others to never give in, nor follow the way of hate or sin!"

Jesus, was one of many 'hands' born of the creator who tries to teach, heal and guide you all away from the abyss ... away from the downward, spiraling 'fall'. More than two thousand years have now passed and 'time' just flows by. Have they all really failed to lead you to your everlasting home?

Of course not ... but it highlights the fact that although you wish for eternity today, not all will feel the same way or strive to achieve this. So, why has it taken so long for humankind to comprehend and accept this? We say it is the doubt, the fear, the greed, and the hate which causes (and has caused) all the imbalance of your karma and misguided desires.

Jesus, a being of divine and brilliant light is one of the 'chosen' throughout time immemorial to try to help mankind to shed the shackles that bind you to the earth-plane floor. He urges you all to open your hearts and say, "I want more!" Yes ... more love, more light, more freedom beyond the limiting aspects of the senses ... indeed, more space to save the human race.

Across every country (and all continents) there has been a special 'one', the one of a kind. Different names and teachers, but they were each born from the same light. All religions, some are diverse and some unifying, but none are wrong for there's not a particular one which resides above another. As long as it is a faith of love, and not one to lead to decay or to hate with clenched fist.

Indeed, there are many other things to be learned, so this is the unique opportunity given to you all. It is time to break free from the world as you know it and live as true 'free' beings of light ... not remain caught or snared in a trap or vice.

At this point the candle flame was approximately eight inches high and it was so beautifully bright.

COMMUNICATION: *David, an image came to you ... of a sticky black mass. Your hands and feet are stuck, as if in mud of this spoilt Earth. Each time you lift a hand or foot to break free it's pulled back and glued to thee. Please listen carefully, for we make a promise from the 'tree'.*

Everyone can break free from this binding density of imbalance upon your souls ... you only have to make it your one true 'goal'. No more, no less, and this is all it will take to escape from life's ups and downs or to leap the seemingly impossible soul's fence.

Hmm, what's that? "If God is so powerful, why doesn't 'He' just clear these days of confusion, banish all decay and disease and all darkness of a living hell?" Is that a question to be followed by another cry of, "Perhaps he's not so powerful after all! God is just a myth created over spans of time and by humankind's own perception?"

Let's go back to when we discussed the 'two opposites', and reiterate this to those who remain doubtful or feel it will be a little too difficult to comprehend. This occurs only because of the gap which exists between the mind and the heart as the wisdom which carries them to a higher level has not quite been bridged. Some may still retort ... "Yet again, what you tell us cannot be proved or substantiated" and "Where is the proof *you* even exist at all and are not just the conception of one person's mind, actions or beliefs."

Okay, those who have this nagging feeling of, 'my mind just cannot comprehend what is being shown or written for us', please place this back into the so called 'past'. We would like to use Jesus as an example again, why would someone of this age and era believe he died upon a cross to save humankind when it happened so, so long ago? Why can thoughts of love and salvation be carried through the millennium to rest in an individual's heart today? How can someone believe in one thing like this when even your most gifted scientists or 'biblical' experts cannot prove beyond doubt that it happened even to this day? This is also the same with all your religions across your globe.

Perhaps it is a touching of your soul's flame by a connection of interior light from someone else's kindness, or maybe it is a page or chapter from the Bible, the Quran or from other works of truth? Do you see? Do you understand? And, if we explain more about ourselves, the same comparison could apply too.

Know that we, the Trans-leátions have evolved with different bodies, different needs and a different 'life'. Also, through many 'times' of space and infrastructure we have grown from the creator's love and light in other ways. We have never said we are better than humanity. Why would we even be here to help you if we had ever felt you were beneath us in any way, shape or form? Indeed, we have grown in wisdom, love, and knowledge in other ways to your own, but we are still from the creator ... created from love and the light which is emitted from God's hearts center.

Forever To Be True

Do you also not think that over the millions and millions of years of our own existence we have never doubted, questioned, or lived the wrong pathway? Process of life ... process of existence and process of learning, it is universal and this must be understood as so. Progress for you as beings of 'light' must follow the new path whereby you recognize you are being given the chance to finally lay your doubts and fears and conceptions to rest.

In their search for answers, people often inquire about passing through different dimensions in terms of universal or galactic evolution, for example moving from the 3rd, or to by-pass the 4th and go to the 5th dimension etc, etc." Those with only a little comprehension and knowledge can become confused or 'lost' within this information and therefore misunderstand what is said. (We will expand on 'dimensions' when it is right to do so further on in this book.) At this time, know it is simply to pass from your present plane of existence to eternity; you're new and beautiful 'home'.

Obviously, one sentence or page cannot fully explain deep-rooted illusions, yet one's life and goal is simplistic ... to live in joy and peace and love in the light. This book however, is put together for you all just to help you along. Ultimately it is you that decide your outcome and fulfillment of your own destiny.

Well David, it is time to go now for your work to attend and your wife to love and to be a friend. We are closer than you think, and just wish to say everything will work out as you and it 'are' meant to be. Hurt and pain, decisions and anguish are all part of your life and your karma needs to be erased. You're searching for the light will bring the true beauty and true gold into your heart.

So, for now, till the pen flows again, love and light we will give and send. Goodbye, in love and peace do trust. P.S. (Reference the structure of this book, do not worry for it will be given when the pen is ready.)

Love and light to you all forever. Thank you from my heart.

CHAPTER THREE: 'CLEARING KARMA AND THE THREE-FOLD FLAME'

Monday 3rd June 1996

Dear Trans-leátions, I thank you for the recent dream. Can the deliverance continue to enable us all to grow? Please let your love, light and wisdom now flow.

COMMUNICATION: *David, we are here and as your vibration rate has increased it is you that we hear.*
The pen is ready and is this for the few indeed, or for the many more to grow and heed. Each day and time the words flow through you, we hope at least one other heart will come and one soul will onward go. Confused? Please do not be.
There are many changes across each town and city. These continue across many Nations and on each and every plane of existence, together with the speeding up of both individual and planetary vibrations too. This will enable everyone to progress and 'Ascend' if they desire it, and if the individual is prepared to sacrifice the hate and greed and the things they do not need.
Perhaps one heart will come to understand and learn new ways of life, living and learning in the presence of the Creator. As one soul 'goes', it also enables others to grow to know the 'light', thus creating a stronger, brighter frequency for other hearts to see, feel and to 'be'.
We have said many times you have your own way to proceed and your own destiny to fulfil and there is a precise time in each of your lives to begin your journey and a desire to climb the 'hill'. Is this a bewildering statement or a simple fact? This choice can be made with a weight lifted or placed as a burden upon your shoulders and back.

Deliverance of Love, Light and Truth

So, we question the individual this very day, do you have the flexibility or do you have a rigid stance? Are you able to alter and change and go with the inner and upper flow of light and truth or do you have the rigidity that keeps you on one route and direction only? You might reply to us in this fashion, "What do you mean? What are you saying? Why question <u>us</u> this day?"

Our reply is this ... why not today, this very minute of this hour? Understand that delaying the ultimate decision or succumbing to thoughts of the 'want' and false greed have no place in an open-heart and mind. Cast them out and please try to rise above them. How do you feel though? Does this bring you tears (of joy) that you will one day cry? Or will it make you feel so down, or make you sit and wonder why?

Where does this now lead you? Are you lost and confused or ashamed and disgraced, in fact so much so you realize that (maybe) an action or thought (either yesterday or today), was slightly out of place? All you can do is to keep trying to improve in the right and only way. You can strive and strive, but you must understand you are on the earth-plane as you have the imbalance of true learning and your life's karma to address.

This said, what you are still made of <u>is</u> perfect though born from the divine! You are the light and the love of the creator and each one of you is attached to the source by a beautiful cord of light. It can not be broken but can in a sense, be released. (The physical self, a denser body is to remain behind, but your 'original' blueprint is retained to Ascend to your special place and home.)

In this chapter, we will continually go back and forth to reiterate the need and different desire to keep your mind and hearts flame growing within the 'white' light and the immense cleansing 'fire'.

We now wish to explain more of the Three-Fold Flame of your heart and to draw away from complex clarifications of what you are. Why make something difficult when it is not and never has been and also never will be.

Okay, the Three-Fold Flame within you is the most beautiful yellow, blue, and pink, do these three colors make you think? Each is entwined by the 'ELOHIM' [27] and as each flame is an individual color it is also constructed and made up of different attribute's and

Clearing Karma and the Three-Fold Flame

elements that are you and imposed upon you. It is these that bring the certain conditions of your life. As you pass through the life you have chosen (on a soul level deciding what must be learned and experienced before you were born into the physical earth -plane) then the Three-Fold Flame both fluctuates and grows.

It consists of 'plumes' of separate flames each within the three flames themselves. As you go through life and overcome each problem, each task and each 'shedding' of negative conditions that encircle and envelop you, these plumes manifest and expand to precisely the same size.

A question we are often asked is, "How many plumes?" The number is universal and as each of us are beings of light, we all have the same. What is different is the diversity and the misshapen and contorted and entangled mess some are in. It is this ugliness that has been attached that needs to be 'spun off' with the raising of the (vibration level), the cleansing of karma. However, it is sufficed to say that each flame contains one thousand 'plumes' and when they reveal their true brilliant colors and completely cleansed they are indeed a most beautiful sight.

The Three-Fold Flame is also a way of acknowledgment and being judged, not by yourself, or us but by the love and light of the creator that is your 'Self'. It is a beacon that radiates and shines within your soul so it highlights your individual progress and achievements to the level you have attained as a child and being of light.

It can also be described as the individual's divine 'Spark'[28] or their 'Holy 'Christ's Flame'. It is precisely 1/16th of an inch in height.

If the color of the Three-Fold Flame is dull or the plumes diminished or misshapen then that soul has much work to be done. The soul will need to change and encompass the light by blocking ill thoughts and actions in their life and by turning within. This will bring in the correct resonance and energy with the one necessary ingredient ... love. In fact, love sustains and ensures its survival.

Once all the plumes of your hearts flame are in the precise position, then you can and you will ascend, make no mistake of that!. However, before this actually happens the Three-Fold Flame is encased in a tube of light. It is the most radiant and brilliant white light from the creator's heart. The cord of Light and of Ascension can only be felt or seen by those who are of the right vibration and frequency of love that has been earned. Indeed, they are those who are over and above the plane of existence that comes from Ascension.

All this may sound complex but in reality, it is not. David, we are going to place a picture/image of a perfect Three-Fold Flame into your mind and heart. For a few moments place down your pen and let the feeling envelop you so you can then draw and describe what you experience.

Phew! That was immense! I could feel myself going into darkness, as if into a deep cave both spinning and spiraling. It was as if I had then become part of a living 'fire', (yet consisting of three flames), not one with heat, but just such love and feeling of immense peace within myself.

It was as if I actually was this fire and had become these outer flames. I stretched out my arm and hand and instinctively 'knew', as if I could sense light 'fragments' of 'blue' (color). They were glistening and glowing with softness and seemed so delicate like the petals of a precious and most beautiful flower. To my right, my hand went into a bright 'pink'. It was as if it was touching, encompassing, and enveloping me. I am the color of the flame!

Somewhat instinctively I moved my head forward and my face piercing the most brilliant 'yellow' I had ever seen. Yes, I was seeing and feeling 'yellow' and I started to become this color. Each separate color then spiraled together and each flame, each plume and each segment of my soul began to be cleansed.

Suddenly a brilliant white light above me came circling down. The three colors became linked, uniformed and fused by it to become one frequency, one vibration, lifting ... spiraling upward. Then whoosh! My mind, my consciousness, my very being become clearer and the experience, the reality, the image (?), was gone. (PICTURE SIX: WITHIN THE THREE-FOLD FLAME).

Everything seemed to stop and I could sense the 'darkness' that had been around the flame had now been pushed 'out'. I

Clearing Karma and the Three-Fold Flame

knew this was the karma, the 'imbalance' shed to one side. The flame of love ... had cleansed this negativity, decay, and the illness of the lower self.

After this, I felt more alive. I understood the yellow flame is the Wisdom of God–the Father/Mother. The blue is for Peace and the Will of God and that pink is for Love, the Love of God. Then the enveloping ray of Light [29] that elevates the soul is the most beautiful and brilliant 'white' light that can ever be imagined. I also came to know they represent many other things too ... that we are all a segment and part of the creator, the Holy Spirit and the Holy 'Christ' self.

COMMUNICATION: *David, it is time to continue now my son. What you have experienced is just part of the splendor of so much more to come through you to be explained and shared. We know for those who read what we have shown here may not comprehend it ... as if this could be in vain, to doubt it and then push it to one side.*

Deliverance of Love, Light and Truth

PICTURE SIX: 'WITHIN THE THREE-FOLD FLAME'

What we ask for are those inner barriers that direct only the plausible thoughts are knocked down for so little is known by humankind of what you actually are and of what you can become. We have said before humankind is still learning DNA and you would be

Clearing Karma and the Three-Fold Flame

far more 'advanced' in technology, peace, and harmony if you could only open your exterior and inner minds and hearts.

You may laugh David but the modern saying of, 'THE TRUTH IS OUT THERE' is absolutely true but do not be blinded by it. Know the truth is within you too and it is here where all reality originates from ... and where it will be forever. Never, ever forget this.

Many, many times in this book and these 'works', you and the reader will feel what is learned is so far fetched you will wonder how you will grow and how you will understand. But just let it flow. As your heart grows so will your mind too and it is with this knowledge that all comprehension, understanding, wisdom will come from. It is the turning to the light and opening up, as a true light 'being' which will enable you to become and be 'one'. Then you can fulfill your individual and collective destiny.

Some information you have already collated can be used if you wish David. It is and always has been your choice too of what is placed in these books/these 'works' with us. You only have to remember whether it will help others and if you feel it is the truth.

Well, today's communication is over my son, but we are here as always and are only a fraction of 'lights' separation away. We hear your thoughts of, 'what do we mean?' This is just a saying my son, just like your 'blink of an eye!' Yes, never to part, never to die. For you truly know now of what, the where and why? You will understand this David.

So goodbye, in love, light and truth from us. In peace and goodwill please trust.

What a wonderful morning. Thank you for your guidance, your love and your truth. Love to you all, from us all.

Thursday 6th June 1996 (8.00 pm)

Dear Trans-leátions, I can sense you drawing closer and feel your your love. It overwhelms me so much ... that I want to cry. I offer my love to you and all the light 'bearers' and 'carriers' across the universe and planes of consciousness, of which we are all part.

Please continue with 'Deliverance' ... for it is beautiful. I wish to

Deliverance of Love, Light and Truth

to learn and grow through your wisdom and your knowledge, just as we all do. Please help and direct us.

I have heard about the 'Violet Fire', can you explain more about this today? Also, how do we cleanse ourselves and increase our desire to do so. Your guidance, encouragement, and your protection too for all I pray.

COMMUNICATION: *David, you are but one speck and flame of love and light that is trying to burn so brightly each and every day and night. You are now learning new information which is continuous and never-ending.*

Each vision, each dream, each book, and each picture bring together another piece of your life's jigsaw and the same goes for all. You are all like a photograph too, one 'negative', together with one 'original' (or positive). The negative ills of karmic imbalance can be cast-off so the positive vibrations and your Three-Fold Flame, your

divine spark can be seen more clearly ... to grow and glow brighter. This is so beautiful to see, and you will to one day. Believe it for it is true.

This belief can start this very minute of this hour of this day, or be put off until your realization when 'Ascension' eventually occurs. So we ask, what is your individual strength and conviction at this present time? We do not and never will chastise, condemn or threaten you but we will always encourage and help you to help yourself. Ultimately (though), it is you and only you that change yourself in this way.

We have said that there are many aspects and avenues and so much to comprehend so take one thing at a time and learn and digest but always do your best. We will never hold the individual or the masses back, but by gradual progress you can grow properly in the right way at your own pace.

For example, a medical student could not learn or understand his 'doctrine' in one day or one term. Likewise, matters of love and light and your own spiritual development are not an overnight procedure. Although we have just referred to it being gradual, please know the chance is now here ... for you to attain the release of your embodiment from the physical and ascend to the creator's heart forever. (i.e. No more re-birth to the physical learning plane [30]). Appreciate you must all work hard to clear the imbalance built over many incarnations of your lives 'experiences'.

Some of this information may be new to some but not for others, or perhaps it has been heard of in similar ways by some who call themselves 'Masters'. Please know there are only the 'Ascended Masters' and no others. People who call themselves this on the earth-plane are not!

Understand too, the individual needs to follow their heart in what they seek and through what they learn, but never be fooled by those who call themselves these words. They cheat and lie both consciously and unconsciously too. Some appear to mean well so listen and learn what their natures and motivations are. Is it money or greed? Do they speak of free will, God's will? Are they masters of one? No, they are masters of none! Many of these souls have lost their way and are unbalanced. They could also be 'fallen Angels', who are trying to tempt you away from your true self, your 'Holy Christ' Self, your higher consciousness and divine spark.

We do not say you should not trust anyone, but by turning within to the truth and love you will find the answers that you seek. In your search, you will also come across many a true heart that will help to expand your love and also lift up your heart. However, they cannot correct your imbalance of karma that you have collected over the millennium as only you can do this in the right way as we have said before.

The Ascended Masters have soul's so pure and are such beautiful beings of light. Jesus, Buddha, Kuthumi, Lord Maitrea, Lord Morya, Mother Mary ... they are numerous but these names and these words are so important, not just as a reference to you, but because of their resonance of light energy. So, when you need to pray and call, giving your decrees, mantra's, fiats, or chants, please understand they have Ascended and are pure love.

The point we are trying to make is not to say or call their names without any true feeling or care within for they may be just words, but in fact they also part of you! At the same time, those who have ascended do not have any manifestation of the 'ego' or project high esteem. They would not rebuke your calls or pleas for help from an open heart, mind or soul. (Or, if you genuinely do not understand or cannot fully comprehend what you are trying to do.)

It is in 'trying' that is so important. It is part of the clearance, for you to be true and not if you say your prayers, affirmation or decrees without feeling. (You know what we mean here). Please do not think these are harsh words. One must understand and question whether there is any point at all ... if you do not believe in what you do. You need to learn and hear these things for the heart and share them with total conviction.

Would a mother kneel to her sick child and whisper, "Get well, I love you" and not mean it? Mm, these words cannot and should not be said without truth from the heart or with hate hiding behind a smile, because they will be adding to the karmic imbalance and debt. Every thought and action either dispels or compels the karmic sanction that withholds you.

It has been understood from the karmic 'board' of the Great White [31] Brotherhood [32] (and all the Ascended Masters and beings of light) that a minimum of 51% of your karmic imbalance is required to be cleared and spun off and erased from your Three-Fold Flame for you to be able to Ascend. The other 49% can continue to be cleared in your non-permanent state, or be balanced whilst in the higher 'octaves' of light vibration.

Raising the resonance of your 'light within' is the same as clearing your karma. By clearing imbalance you raise your inner soul's rate of vibration and vice versa, and through living in peace, harmony, and trust in faith too, then this will also contribute towards your goal. This can be simplified even further, live as one and God is (in) you just as you are part of God. David, your mind has wandered and the connection strained. We sense you are a little tired, shall we continue?

Please, for a short while longer.

COMMUNICATION: *Also note, to Ascend is your 'birth right'. It is your right to return to the creator's heart to reside as 'beings' of light in your new home, your new 'plane' of existence, and the communal plane for the light eternal.*

Can you think of something you have wanted so much on the earth-plane? (Place yourself in many people's current state of thinking.) Perhaps a new car or a house or this or that or the other. How much effort does the individual put into their work to pay for these things or to achieve what is only the 'material' ... a fabrication of denseness and only a fleeting pleasure in time and space?

You could reply there is nothing new with what we say regarding materialism but what we wish to place into perspective is that when you want something so much it tends to envelop your whole being and your world ... well, simply multiply that same 'desire' and effort to what is really needed and required and then place it in your soul's flame. Then you will achieve fulfillment and your inner goal to become what you can become. To live, love and forever truly be 'ONE'.

Well my son it is time to rest now. We will go over many more aspects, including the Violet Fire/Flame in more detail. Goodbye for now. In love, light, and peace, please trust forever.

Sorry for being tired during this communication. Love to you all too, forever in love and light.

Wednesday 12th June 1996 (6.40 pm)

Something is so very strange today. Perhaps I have let you down in some way? A feeling that although I have looked for and tried to feel these 'new' experiences somehow, I may abandon you. Why do I feel this?

I know I have such a long way to go and so much to learn. As such, I now re-affirm I will never inflate my ego in what I have experienced or through what I can share. We are all 'one', all part of God, our creator. So please continue, for my heart and mind are open for your love and light and truth. I love and bless you all and I will, forever.

COMMUNICATION: *David, as you feel the 'peace' envelop you, please understand you are 'free'. You have free will, together with God's will every day and in every way ... as you all do. Every* *child, son and daughter of God are love and light, so how could you offend us, my son? We do not think you have, because you continue to search for the reality of you. Each of you who open can never offend the truth above, below, and also within you.*

Your search and goal will always be infinite, but once in the light of your new plane of existence, (your new home), you will remain permanently embodied in this higher vibration to continue into eternity in peace and love. Yes indeed, always, and forever.

Do you remember when we first acknowledged your call for greater wisdom and for love and light? It was the two lights, two Stars, a symbol of 'us'. Now of course, you know so much more regarding our connection to the true source, but at first you did not. It was your endeavor to search and learn that enabled you to understand and broaden your mind and hearts horizon, and so it will always be.

Please know this information together with new understanding will come in many ways, shapes and forms and also from many teachers in many places. It is you; the individual who will follow and continue in an area of knowledge and comprehension that feels right for you and you alone.

What would be the purpose and use of someone following their brother or sister (of light) without trying to comprehend and learn for themselves first? Conversely, we say how can you dismiss something out of hand as farcical or leading your heart astray if you do not place any effort or your entire being into it?

Did Buddha, Gautama, Jesus, or any Ascended Master state you would succeed in a day, a week, or a month? No, only for you to open to the light, the beautiful light that is God. You are God as you are God's light. You are all so beautiful, but are often hidden in darkness and imbalance from past life experiences and karma ... which is one of the same. The only dispensation is this unique opportunity to change in this lifetime. Yes a unique opportunity for your soul's journey to make the 2nd, 3rd or 4th wave [33] of Ascension. As always, this choice and task and the chance is yours alone to take.

As the East meets West and 'religions' of many time frames on your Earth come to a head, (in difficult trials of your

Clearing Karma and the Three-Fold Flame

lifetime), then so must each of you overcome the disappointments and setbacks suffered too. This is not new to ask you to cast pain, disappointment and disillusionment to one side but now come out of your shell, do not shy away and hide'.

You must be yourself in everything you say and do and try not to hurt any other being of light or try to 'fool'. To cheat or tell lies blinds your own light into a veil of darkness and also promotes decay. It will lead your physical to cry out when it dies and fades away. A shock of realization instead ... and not the immediate guiding hand to the promised land. (We do not mean to frighten or scare anyone but aim to increase your awareness and 'inner' insight, to move you forward and enlighten.)

Well, now let us move on from this track of thought and come full circle to the one or nought. We will soon start a new chapter David, but we wish to conclude with a little more information on the Violet Fire, along with the desire to become 'whole' and of so much more inside your hearts flame.

We had described earlier of how important it was to change for the better as an individual, as a family member, community 'teacher' or in whatever place or position you hold in your workplace or society. This is not in the sense of an enhancement or promotion but in the sense of a glowing light and emitting the radiance from 'within'. You're inner light and your glowing Three-Fold Flame is that divine spark of your soul, your Christ consciousness. It will glow and become brighter and higher as you progress forward.

The Violet Flame (fire) is around you at all times, but you cannot see it and you cannot touch it! Inside is where you can truly feel it. It is with your inner self you connect to the Holy presence that is above and all around you and everywhere in existence. Okay, you may now ask, 'How large is your Violet Flame/fire?' It is as large as you want it to become. Indeed, you could imagine yourself as the Violet fire itself or you can project your thoughts out (further) to envelope your family, your home, even your city or nation, the whole planet, or even across every plane of existence. You can place the Violet Flame/fire anywhere you wish. Please know it can even cast out the karmic imbalance of all and this is no trick.

Deliverance of Love, Light and Truth

The Violet fire will cleanse every light being and soul and this should also be the overall 'goal'. You must cleanse and clear your own imbalance from your very being You are also able to help or pray for those around you and every being of light and all elemental life too. This is very important.

Comprehend it is the individual's priority to succeed in Ascension for as we have also said before, due to karmic imbalance, it can be hard enough even for yourself. N.B.: The process has and always will be simple, but your karma and life experiences as well as your interaction with others makes it difficult. The reason why we now discuss this is to reiterate that so many others can be helped at the same time too.

In the past when the burden has been too much to cope with then the negative vibrations the Elemental(s)[34] have had to carry exploded into devastation across your globe causing the extinction of many cultures and civilizations. Know that the 'life' of Atlantis and Leamura were dissolved and consumed this way. The burden of humankind's past and it's sins reflecting in the need of the Elemental(s) to cast off their heavyweight of your activities and life's ills. This is not condemnation, but factual events with a realization of possible duplication. It is God's warning deep inside you all and this is already known. So indeed, it is time for a change and to address the imbalance.

In times of lifting up your light, place the flame of Gods love around you. During prayer, meditation or your mantras and decrees let your spoken word cast out the ills and lift the light vibration to a higher frequency. Your voice and your call through your throat chakra (energy point) will have the greatest effect on the change that is required. The light of the Ascended Masters will hear it and the call will not be revoked or pushed aside. It cannot and will never ever be.

Your commands and callings will be heard and carried across the planes and the universe and will lighten the darkness ... and also give strength to the weak. This will help and strive to clear the karmic debts placed upon yourselves over the millennium, both by yourself and by the sins and darkness of negative imbalance.

Remember; do not fear. What you sense as fear is your

Clearing Karma and the Three-Fold Flame

realization of the unknown. So, by turning 'within' to your true light source of life, you will overcome all ills and doubt. The Violet Flame will shed and erase your karmic imbalance ... your yesterday, the past week, the last month and so on and so forth and then your future imbalance too!

Only by your perseverance and continued growth will you truly come to see what is in place, then true love will beam through your heart, your physical and across your soul's 'face'. It will envelop your very core and your soul will cry out, 'Please God, more?' The love that awaits you (and you can often sense and almost touch) is beyond comprehension. It is never spurned or turned away from love that will last for an eternity and a day. How could the Father/Mother God turn its back on its child? The creator can never do this and never will.

Likewise, as on the earth-plane, have you ever recalled an abandoned child who has been left on a cold or lonely step? Deep, deep down in the heart of the parent is a love that is bound together so strongly, nothing can erase it and nothing can break it. On the surface, this may not be recognized because of the circumstances and karmic situation around both of these souls to make that event happen. (This statement is not an excuse for it is the truth and a 'reality' that occurs in every country, your world over.)

Only by inwardly cleansing yourself can the events of the physical life and world be rectified. You can and will succeed. You just have to believe in yourself and to trust your God ... our God ... for all life is given from and created by God.

David, we need you to draw and describe the next picture so all can see, then a new chapter will begin where we let you experience new things and explain more about the Etheric planes and higher 'octaves' of light too. This will also include the 'Lords of the Seven Rays', their colors and their definition of love and light. Are you intrigued? Open your eyes of your heart and mind and envisage the Violet Flame my son, then all will be revealed for you are part of us and you are all also part of the one true source.

At first I wasn't quite sure what to expect or experience. Then suddenly everything became clear apart from the outside edges of my 'minds eye'. This appeared like a beautiful 'haze' of soft white light. (Just as if I was staring through a photographer's lens used for romantic wedding pictures). This was quite apt because there was an overwhelming feeling of 'union', a wedding ceremony of sorts. A soul now unifies its light with the light of God's presence. (The Bible calls this the 'Alchemical Marriage' – whereby the soul is always female whether or not it is in a male or female 'body'.)

On this occasion came an image of a man, naked (and yet not?) within a flame. A circle of violet color enveloped him both reflecting and pulsing around his 'Three-Fold Flame' in the centre of his body. He then seemed to walk up a step and stand in a Violet Chamber of flames. This was so beautiful. Flecks of brilliant white and then violet light were intermixing, sparkling magnificently. Oh, the beauty of this is so hard to describe.

My eyes, heart and mind seemed to be as one with his for a moment. It was as if I was looking outwardly through him. Suddenly, I am viewing from the outside, looking inward again. I then gazed upon a spiraling light, (like a helix or DNA pattern) as if an inner silver cord [35] was gleaming like crystal. The Violet then disappears and everything is just white. Then up and up and up into a sphere of brilliant white light, and then came a heart enveloped by a multitude of colors. All were so brilliantly clear and so magnificent! (PICTURE SEVEN: 'THE VIOLET FLAME AND THE HIGHER SELF'). Phew!

COMMUNICATION(Cont.): *Okay David, it is time for us to go but we will speak and feel your heart again soon. In love and light and peace do trust. Love to you all, always from us. Goodbye.*

Thank you from my heart for this incredibly special experience. Love and light to you all. Forever. N.B.: I had also learned this picture was so very important for it basically represented your past, present and future too. The inner 'teacher', a mediator between God and 'Man' which overshadows the lower self, was the past. In the centre was the Higher-Self, the Christ consciousness, this was the present and the 'I AM' presence above, i.e. God, represents the future.

The lower self [36] consists of the soul evolving through the four planes of matter using the vehicle of the four lower bodies, both to balance karma and fulfil the 'divine plan'.

These three parts or elements correspond with and to the Trinity Father (always including Mother), the Son and the Holy Spirit whose sacred fire is indicated in the enfolding Violet Flame. Therefore, you are the disciple on the path. Your soul is the non-permanent aspect of being is made permanent through the ritual of Ascension!

PICTURE SEVEN: THE VIOLET FLAME AND THE HIGHER SELF

CHAPTER FOUR: 'COLORS'

So much has been going on in my personal life. It is so strange, even when you have so much love around you, you can often still feel insecure or doubtful of your life and its meaning.

This is weird, as I know I have been helped through my prayers and decrees and my meditations. So, before the next chapter and 'communications' truly begin, I would like to share two recent experiences that lifted my heart, which was feeling so 'blue'. Is this a color (or a feeling) that right now, you too, are going through?

Friday 14th June 1996 (5.00 am)

During my prayers, mantras and decrees I experienced the most incredible feeling within myself. I had been sitting in an upright position; palms of my hands facing upward and they started to tremble. Not on the outer physical sense, but as if 'inside'.

On many occasions when I use crystals and also through healing, I have been overwhelmed with the heat and energy connecting and flowing with such love through me, but this was totally different.

The two small chakra's (one in each palm) seemed to paralyze my hands and lower arms. This may sound strange but it was not painful in any way, just a feeling of an unbelievable sense of power, love and energy flowing into me. My whole body began to sense a vibration shift, speeding up which brought peace and contentment within and around me. It was truly a wonderful feeling!

Monday 17th June 1996 (7.05 – 7.25 pm)

I have also decided to share a meditation with you all. It highlights and explains what the Trans-leátions mean by turning within and through saying your prayers, decrees and in the asking of help for the Light ... which will come if your heart is truly open.

As I said a little earlier, I feel I have many challenges in my personal life, yet I feel selfish too, because these concerns would pale into insignificance against disease, death and hunger of so many. Though I do know this, my heart still aches when unhappiness comes and my tears fall. This is another reason for this meditation to be included and shared with you all.

MEDITATION: I had asked for Jesus to come and help me. I said an invocation to Him for His love and light to draw close. My mind suddenly seemed to blur over and then, high above my consciousness.

A door to 'Heaven' then opened and a beautiful and radiating golden light shone in every direction. It moved towards me and a figure, just an outline at first, emerged from it. There standing before me was Jesus! (Yet I could not understand how I could 'see' through—and at—this brilliant light. I moved even closer and knelt before Him, bowing my head. Jesus then spoke to me, but not through a 'voice' for I could feel Him in my heart.

Jesus: "You come to me my son, but do not kneel before me for I am part of you, just as You are part of me and this will always, always be. We are both of God, love, and light, each and every day and night. Arise, my child."

Suddenly it was like I had become a sparkle, a fragment of light and I fell into His open hand. He spoke again and I could sense and 'hear' his sweet, tender, and loving 'voice' within me.

Jesus: "Come inside with me. In light, do you see your many friends, family, teachers and guides?"

I looked and looked, 'I do not Father, I cannot see them', I replied.

Jesus: *"David, do you look with your eyes, or do you feel and see with your heart?"*

A wonderful realization overcame me and many tears began to fall just like a beautiful 'waterfall' cascading over a crystal bed of 'light'. Such love, a feeling of immense love and peace filled my very being.

Jesus: *"You feel the way you do over many things for simple reasons. Yes, they are important (as are so many), yet you also simply forget. How old does one have to be to see the light? Know that you all open like flower buds only when you are ready too. You cannot force the petals with impatience or misunderstanding my son, no matter how much you feel your love will do so. Those around you, like all, will do so in their own time. You can love and stay with this love. It is up to you and always has been. Is this your karma or not? Only through your heart and how you feel and act is important. Remember that it is always up to you too. Just follow your dream and all your dreams will come true. For to follow the dream will mean your return, to your one true home."*

With these words, I knew I then had to return,

Jesus spoke again: *"Just believe and succeed in all that you do. It is your time to go now, my son."*

With a soft breath, he blew me from his hand, like a white petal of a flower bud in the wind. I cried out, "Please Father, I do not ... I do not want to go!" But I knew I could not stay. I could sense myself being 'grounded' back into my physical. My tears rolled down my face as I sat and cried. It was as if my very soul was torn in two, yet strangely, I felt so complete. Oh, this was so very strange indeed.

I prayed, 'Thank you dear Jesus and to you all in the light. From my heart, I give my love to you. Forever I will send it, until I am permanently home. I then recalled what Jesus had once said, 'I am the door, I am the light and the way'.

Perhaps this comes to my mind right now because the Trans-leátions re-iterate this, both to guide you and put everything else into perspective. Remember you are the light and you are also the door, so never hide or try to seek anymore. Love and light to you all.

Monday 24th June 1996 (11.00 am)

I call from my heart for your love, light, protection and guidance. My dear friends and family of light, please come and connect with me in strength, love and wisdom so that the 'Deliverance' may flow from you to the hearts, souls and minds of the many.

Dear Millanderer and Zerrog, please listen to my words of this pen and let it flow in 'love' once again.

COMMUNICATION: *We are here my son. Your light shines and emanates upward and bursts through the clouds of confusion, never an intrusion upon time or the elements of love and light. It is like an arrow, shot from one heart to another blazing through the galaxy and looking for love and eternal light's color.*

The book is opened once again and each page is to reveal a poem, a song, and a picture or simply words. 'Something for everyone' is what we hope will be heard across many towns and cities and nations, guiding and delivering to 'he' who wishes to open and connect to the true source of love and light, our God, our creator.

Let each page flow and grow. All will then know the information and guidance that is to be revealed so the outer layer of darkness, hate and sin can then be peeled. For there inside remains your golden and brilliant white glow, your true life 'source' and beautiful true soul.

Okay, today is the start of a new chapter, which we will simply call 'COLORS'. This is because color is universal and is emitted and perceived by many various life forms and existences and not just by

Colors

your earthly eyes alone. We will also discuss the Lords of the Seven Rays, for they can also be said to be guardians of each color(s) purification and emittance, which was a task given to them by the creator). First of all, we should go back to basics and talk about your combined color ray of your rainbow, which is so beautiful, but is it unique?

Please know color encompasses us all with many attributes and with an enormous potential that lies within us. It is universal because it is in everything you say, do and feel and what you are too. Know that each color is a vibration, both within and 'out'. So, within a Rainbow, there is the combination of color, which goes far beyond the fable and the 'pot of gold' as it contains much truth for whom it beholds. What do we mean by this?

In its essence, its core is the peace and purification of truth, love and light and the manifestation, as you perceive is only a visual one. Yet, when your heart and soul becomes one and truly opens, you can feel the higher resonance with its sweet frequency which pierces your being ... enhancing the love with hope and peace within you.

Of course, your earthly atmospheric conditions produce the scene and it captivates the viewer. Remember though, the source from where it came from and also the Sun born from the creator. For without the Sun you would not see your 'colors' at all and you would not exist as you do at this time.

When you also hold a crystal (clear quartz for example), does a rainbow fragment within it? Can you see that crystals <u>are</u> light and also contain the colors of the universe? Some may think they are solid but they are not. They vibrate at their own special frequency, as does everything and every living thing.

Know those upon Atlantis had forgotten this fact, that their crystals were their light and power and the reality inside of them was misused! We see that 'modern' man has electrical motors and power generators and is now moving on to higher technology such as lasers. However, has great progress really been made? We will not judge you for it is you who will need to decide this for yourselves.

So, color is 'vibration' and frequencies are combined both holding and releasing and emanating as and when it is required in whatever capacity you can think of. If you allow yourselves time to notice these vibrations you can instantly feel the benefits as you can feel stronger, more positive, and more 'alive'.

As you know, if you take the spectrum (or prismatic colors), then make a disc containing each one (in a different segment) and spin it at a fast rate, they all disappear ... you can only observe white. Therefore, white light is the highest vibrating color (and 'fire' substance) in the cosmos and creation. The 'rays' vibrate at a lower frequency and hence they appear as different colors. These frequencies and vibrations also have a sound or 'keynote' too.

The primary colors and the 'seven' (a magical number), are emitted from Heaven. They also bind and entwine and hold all the frequencies in place. They are linked in so many more ways than you can think. For example, one connection is that the 'Seven Rays' link to various chakra's too, so let's take one at a time to see if you will understand and share in the defined love and beauty.

RED. This frequency, this color has many shades. Perhaps it could now be seen as symbolic of death, of blood and of anger entwined as one, but only if you have lowered yourself and are not ready to 'become'. Red is for energy, but with the lowest vibration. Yet, when mixed with the white light, its frequency and vibration then becomes 'pink' [37], perhaps not a fire but within the heart a real desire? So, of the red to pink, does it make you stop and think?

It can encompass and envelop you like a rod of iron or a sheet of steel and it can protect and give you physical strength in the battle to fight the ills and decay that sometimes surround or (do) penetrate you. You can become this energy and source if you need it within or around your body or your mind.

ORANGE. This frequency can be the source of vitality, light and heat so fill your mind, your body and your soul with this flowing color of 'Assimilation' for your whole being. Think and feel it for a moment. Yes... become orange. Breathe it in and take its traits of energy and vibration for this is what you possibly need. Place the book down if you wish to try to 'become'. Perhaps the feelings that overcame you are soft and gentle, or were a powerful rush to the mind that enabled you to feel, to know as one of a kind.

Orange, is universally known as a link to the core giving a craving within for more of what you need, whether that need is physical, emotional, mental or spiritual. The frequency and vibration stimulate and assimilates the divine essence of what you are lacking within and around you and in your life. Orange will come to you if you need it for it will be part of 'change' as and when you require it.

And of course, as in any color that you clothe yourself in, wear it when you feel you need it. This can happen subconsciously too when you get dressed for the day for a color maybe chosen because you require it around you. (Color therapy is well-known so we do not wish to expand or go over what knowledge you already have on this).

As this information came through me, I felt so warm knowing there was so much love all around me. The candle flame in front of me began to weave and dance side to side like a magical wand of light. It was so beautiful.

COMMUNICATION: *We detract for a moment now my son, for as we watch and see the light emanate from thee, there are beautiful spirals of hope and joy. If you could only see them as they truly are (and what you all are) and what you consist of, then you would surely shed a fountain of tears.*

You are all Gods wonderful children of light and just as you differ in the colors of your skin, the language of your voice and individual character, so the light changes within and around you all. But at the very core, you are all the same and are no more and no less than one another.

When you think of yourselves as the children of God, then you can bring things into perspective in many areas of your lives. However, you may feel you are insignificant sometimes and that whatever you do cannot possibly change the way that people think or alter their actions too.

When you realize that you are a part of God (and that power of love and light is within you), you can change and unify together and can accomplish anything you want to. World peace, food, and clothes for every nation ... all these can be achieved and it's only the negativity and darkness around and within you that is holding you back to discover the truth of 'you'.

By changing the color of 'negative' thoughts and feelings to the brighter shades of love, you will increase the level of vibration in yourself and everywhere that life exists. So expand and believe your individual and collective thoughts are carried far beyond the home in which you live, to cross the planes of consciousness and existence to the home of billions of life-forces and energies across the universe. Your mind, heart and soul are as big or as small as you believe it to be, or more importantly, what you want it to be. (Also of course what it can do for everything around you and far beyond you too).

When you contemplate beyond your so-called chores or problems of your life you will know everything is connected. Each being, each soul, each color is a vibration and frequency, perhaps on different levels ... but all are part of the true source. It is the understanding of this that can enable you to utilize 'color' in thought and perception far beyond what you see with the physical eye.

YELLOW [38] so radiant and beautiful is the Sun and Son of God who emanates power, life, light and heat and also eternal wisdom. But what does yellow signify to you? Perhaps it is the sunshine color, penetrating and filling you with warmth and love. Does it make you feel good about yourself? On a bright and clear day if you look directly at the Sun with your physical eyes it can hurt or blind and vibrate inside your mind and head.

Strangely, this sensation resembles the way darkness within can similarly make you feel. It is subconsciously trying to trick you to turn away from the light (and Gods love) and in pushing you away you will feel confused or even used. Yet, when you close your eyes and lay in the Sunlight, you will feel the warmth upon your face and body. It is completely different because you feel good, you are content, happy ... and 'alive'. Is this really just stimulation or a simple state of mind?

In reality, consider the golden Sun as truly part of the creator and part of you too. Its light enables living things to grow and flourish and to seek upward and higher and higher towards it, as if to try to touch it. Likewise, the Son [39], as 'Gods love' is also sustaining you and your plants and animals and all life on your plane of existence and planet. Just like the Sun, without Gods love permanently in your heart, you will die and lose your identity as a soul. David, you ask to pause in your mind. What is it?

Yes I recall in Pathway how you mentioned the casting out of the soul, which intrigued me. Not to detract from this chapter and this book but can you explain what you meant by this, particularly for those who wish to understand more of what you have just described. I feel that there is a link to this information.

COMMUNICATION: *Okay, we had explained before that it is only the creators decision and choice regarding what happens 'eternally' to your soul. We mentioned the emptiness and the drifting of a soul into eternity, with only the potential of an 'if and when' that the creator may decide to allow the soul to 'experience the truth of light' again.*

There is a fundamental difference to what we now say. When you cross over from the physical plane, your life, your light (vibration/ frequency rate) and everything you have ever been and had continued to be is known within the soul. Then, there will be a decision made ... with God. A judgement day? Could the worst possible scenario for the individual be the loss of their identity (memory) as a soul and being of light?

Imagine for a moment you are many thousands of 'years' old and have internally stored all your experiences and knowledge as memories over that time. Then, with a blink of an eye you do not know who or what you are. This would mean that you are returned as a fragment of the light's infrastructure and not as an 'individual soul'.

The nearest pain and anguish you could relate to this on your earth- plane is total memory loss and missing such is well documented. Find out for yourself and you will learn of the frustration, pain, and anguish of what those (who even with a partial memory loss) and their close family goes through. Multiply this by an unimaginable quantification and you may just realise what it could feel like. (Throughout our search to help many civilizations and planets this loss of identity has occurred.)

Deliverance of Love, Light and Truth

David, another thought emanates from you. That it is slightly off 'track', but you think and feel of what and why? People may say, "How can God do or contemplate doing such a thing to a being, a child of 'His' light? Please remember you are the child and all children of light are loved beyond comprehension. Never forget this! We reply with a question, 'Does a Father/Mother never punish or reprimand their child in any way whatsoever?'

On your physical plane, it can be a crossed word, or a restriction imposed of some kind, perhaps a loss of a privilege? (Or sometimes a physical force is used.) Again we ask a question in return, 'Can you say God is not able to control 'His' children (or have the right to) as you do over your physical child?' Some may say that God did not or does not ever interfere with progress etc, so we ask, 'At what point would you say to your child', "Do not do that for it is wrong!" Aha, that is your own jurisdiction and your own free will is it not? Yes or no?

People have also cried out, "Why God, do you allow such pain and suffering? He can't be a loving God if He allows this to happen." What is misunderstood here is that in the 'beginning' (all) asked our God, our creator, and our Father/Mother to give us free will to be co-creators with Him. He gave us this 'gift'. Yes 'free-will' to go out into the vastness of the universe and 'create' according to his will. (i.e. Being co- creator with God). However, after a time, the reason for 'being' was forgotten. Wilfulness set in and the choice to act through one's ego, which was not according to the overall 'divine' plan for light and for the life that was given.

Hence humankind then entered into a much denser sphere until it arrived into the 'physical' embodiment. Most forget (and continue to do so) that they have a Father/Mother God in whose likeness and image they were made. But you may now realize that Gods 'laws' are all-merciful. This is because of the karma (this negativity) that has been made by the individual and the masses, has now been given the opportunity through the law of 'rebirth' (what is being reaped for what has been sown) can now be cleared.

Humankind can return to their first estate and make their Ascension and become immortal 'Sons and daughters' of God. Therefore, may it be understood it is (and was) this blatant misuse (through evolution and existence) of the free will, that everything must now return to God's Will. Please feel and understand what we hope you can accept inside yourself. Okay, we hope that clarifies your query, so we will now continue with the 'Colors' and the theme.

GREEN [40]. It has many shades from almost jade, but it can be so pale with a hint of lime. It can heal and nurture both heart and mind with a frequency so sweet; it seems to sing just like a musical chime. It is the color of 'nature' and contains the nurturing of the creator's hand, revealing life and giving balance across each land that enables us all to understand.

Like a conductor, a receiver of energy directly from the source, all 'green' can be so serene. What does one feel when you walk through a forest or enchanted meadow if you simply open your heart? Every cell of your body can be filled with the vibration of Gods magical wand of life and art, yes beauty in every stone and rock, in every leaf and in every blade of grass. Have you ever stopped and wondered, or have you ever thought to ask?

Some may consider what we describe as too simplistic, and of course, we would not have it any other way. Yet for others it will seem so hard to accept or comprehend (at first) but in the reality of 'opening up' to the light, everything is really so simple made. If you just take in the beauty God has created, you can realize from the experience and through and with <u>all</u> of your senses.

If you feel ill or depressed immerse yourself in 'green'. It will soothe and re-vitalize you and give you the realization and the strength to pass life's 'tests'. You can then overcome and go on to feel the joy of healing that is universally seen. It could be 'within' you require to be made well in the love and light and once you have recognised this is so, then everything on the outer you (your body) will be all right. It is the illness and stress of the mind and heart which manifests and decays bodily parts. Such negativity and hate are part of these ills that explode and overflow to 'show' and reveal this.

Yes indeed, love and light can be so swallowed up by the lower vibrations and murky colors of both deceit and pain that it makes raising yourself exceedingly difficult. So if you feel so bad or lonely, or feel you have had enough, just turn within to the light and its loving touch. If you cannot, go to where there is 'green' for it will help you to appreciate life and feel Gods love again, and there too you will find the truth in what we mean.

David, it is time to go now my son, and we thank you for our 'time' together. Thank you for thoughts just now, we feel your love and peace too. Goodbye for now, the pen will flow again soon. In love and light, we trust.

At this point the candle's flame was so bright and beautiful. As if it was giving out twice as much light. Thank you from my heart for being in and being part of my life.

Friday 28th June 1996 (5.30 pm—6.30 pm)

Dear Trans-leátions, please continue chapter Four and 'Colors' with your words of love and light for us all. I can now feel you drawing closer to me.

The peace it brings is so vibrant and precious. It is like turning on a tap and the love flows out is from the eternal source. It feels as if I am being touched with an everlasting feeling of joy both by day and night. Please place the inner-dictations and words on these pages, so they may last throughout the new and forthcoming ages.

COMMUNICATION: *Yes, simple words of truth my friend being conveyed with the flow of your pen.*

We see that sheets of rain have covered your 'home' for most of the day and this water ... this 'life' is being given freely to the earth. This 'life-force' contains love and in every place of existence falls 'upon' every plane in one form or another. For a moment, please forget about your scientific explanations of the forming of 'H2°' and its molecular structure. Water is built upon skies and seas of 'blue' and also great pools of cosmic energy, which emanate from way up above and below you.

BLUE [41]. It can be found in every place and in every rock, its vibration constant just like the ticking of your 24-hour clock. As you look into the clear blue sky or across an ocean, the energy contained cannot be harnessed or manufactured into a confined space, though it can truly sustain you all, yes every single 'race'.

Does it bring feelings of the cold or is this just in your mind? And do you have a sense of anticipation and glow, to find it is but one of a kind? From the softest, palest hue to the spellbinding, enveloping radiance of its deepest variation, ask yourself, what does the color blue really mean to you?

Please understand it is a color, a frequency for each and every one of you. It is nurturing, guiding and protecting and each blue ray that manifests represents a different part of you. It cools and dampens the fire of anger in your heart and is there to soothe the tenseness of a tired mind. Its uses are many and it is there for whoever requires it for their own specific needs. Remember, all you have to do is to be still and 'open' up.

It can be mystifying too. Place your open hand into a bucket of water from the beautiful sea and then pull it up. It flows through your fingers and cannot be held; yet its energy is grasped and its love and strength retained within because you have touched a true source of love from God. As the droplets glide between your fingertips and fall from the palm of your hand, it returns to its origin, not born from any earthly source or made in any land. It is energy, a life-force indeed and it is part of the creator that will <u>always</u> remain free.

So, when in troubled times and you feel enclosed, immerse yourself in the color blue and you will feel the 'letting go' from the burdens that try to tie you down to all that is wrong and are around. We make a promise ... in the 'true' blue, you cannot frown and you will never, ever drown.

We have paused for a moment David as you contemplated the next color, Indigo. Why is this so? We know there have been many works across your earth-plane on these important colors and rays of light that flow from the creator (and from within) so please do not worry or be overly concerned. Learning should be fun and is just a 'tool', but only if you truly feel it doesn't belong to any fool. Any doubt and in carrying those opinions matter only to those with closed minds and hearts. They currently feel separated from the light but will one day recognize they are indeed part of the eternal source and ever-lasting God and 'His' love.

INDIGO [42]. This is a unique mixture of color/vibration. It forms a special glow that's 'combined' for it is not alone. We will reveal more on this soon but for now David we know that it is time for you to go. There are things that you need to do, but remember we love you (and you all) and will miss you too. 'till next time the pen flows in love and light, be at peace. Do trust as you are always one and are always part of us.

Bless you, all and thank you too from your friend and son, David.

Monday 1st July 1996

Heavenly Father/Mother, Great White Spirit our creator, I pray for love, light, peace, and truth. Please watch over me and allow words of hope, encouragement and wisdom will shine through the Transleátions and this pen. Please continue with 'Colors.' Bless you all in love and light.

COMMUNICATION: *My son, we are here, and we hear your call ... yes, all for one and one for all!*

We will continue with Indigo (and where we last left off) in a moment, but we need to mention a forthcoming chapter. Not of this book, but a change of thought overcoming each and every nation. Make no mistake, vibration and frequencies are being raised amidst the darkness and sin that overhangs like a hangman's noose, but the 'light' is stronger and it is going to cut this free and all loose.

Contemplation is occurring in every soul and in every light both by day and by night. Some of you see, feel or think in new ways and others are beginning to search the inner and outer waves of their own frequencies of light. This is reflected and seen by new 'eyes' upon a book, a picture or perhaps a poem. Perhaps a scene of nature created by the universal artist of love and light, the creator, our God, your God ... the one God.

Do not dwell on the so-called bad things that come into your lives, let them go and do not think twice. Changing yourself is the way to go, and by doing so you will then start to 'know'. You will see the door of light opening before you and your heart, and in the new direction, the seeds of love have been sown.

There will shortly be an event upon your plane of existence that will bury a myth laid dormant in your history. It is (and will be) something to behold by the many or perhaps just by the few? It will lead to greater confidence in forging the new belief and purpose of your individual and global Pathway and Ascension trail. What could this be? Upon which date and also the how and why and when?

These are all questions of the outer mind. Please listen and feel this within, for we do not mean in these ways. There will be a message understood by those with frequencies of light who are growing and radiating together and are becoming brighter each day. It is inside the heart where this universal message of love will be received.

This message will be pushed outward with greater love and light. As if it has been conducted and relayed from a charge of pure energy, indeed from the creator direct. (Which is where we first started today). Yes a link and a connection. One and for all, to hear and feel and to participate within the call. Those who receive it will know exactly what we speak of. Perhaps <u>you</u> will experience it? Believe us and more importantly believe in yourself.

Some of those who read this chapter may feel we are often going back and forth, touching upon one thing, then another and then back again. (Why?) This is easier to comprehend when you realize everything is connected. What we have just spoken of is the connection and the power to the Three-Fold Flame of the heart. Are the energies and your divine spark not a frequency of a special vibration and also of color?

Indigo to continue with now. It's frequency and color are associated with the unfolding of spiritual understanding and links with imagination and intuition. It has a unique vibrancy. Immerse your mind for a brief moment and reflect upon it. Reflect being an appropriate word because its properties are (and act) like a mirror!

It has different characteristics, with rebounding energy and its structure contains, dual frequencies, which are a perfect match. You could place an object into its vibration/energy and you could see two images, or none at all! A *'mirage'* of light that can elude but never frighten ... as it soothes the most perturbed heart and mind.

If you look upon a rainbow, would you say Indigo is further or nearer the curve? Aha, is it the outer or inner curve? (Once more the confusion or illusion?) Likewise, if you were to take a second look upon the picture of the Ascension Flame and the I AM presence above, you will see concentric rings of light emanating from the Heavens, the I AM and God presence itself. As Indigo is the farthest away, does this mean that it is less or more important than the other colors/vibrations?

The vibration levels may be different, but this is all. Please know each color/vibration is as important as each other are. This is the way it has always been and will be forever. It will become clearer to you in the mind and in your heart, for in reading this today is only just the start.

You need to read, learn, and digest these so your progress can continue and also enable you to pass the creators love and light Ascension *'test'*. A test that each of you can take on a soul level if you wish to. No force, no pain other than what you, your karma and karmic lessons have chosen to play. The lower frequencies and the ills and sins of others who do not turn to the light are the ones who are creating the havoc and intend on having a *'field'* day. All of you have the ability to stop this, and you can win if you want and desire to.

David, today's message is to be cut short. More will arrive when you are ready. Go and relax and take a break. Know that opportunities are coming your way and you will make the most of them if your heart stays true. Never doubt and never fear for the truth is in you too. Love and light to you all. Goodbye for now and in peace and love do trust. Go forward and onward. We finally say, *is this* a must?

Very interesting indeed. Thank you for what you have sent today. As always love and light to you too ... from your 'son', David.

Saturday 13th July 1996 (2.45 pm)

First of all, I turned the cassette player on to listen to some relaxing music. I sat down in front of the candle I had lit as usual and prayed to open my heart for the love and light to flow through me. Suddenly an image/scene came through, wow! This was much stronger than any visualization!

It began with me viewing the Earth and it looked so beautiful as it was bathed in shades of an almost translucent green and blue. Suddenly, a golden cross began to shine brilliantly above it! Rays of magnificent light beamed down from the cross, enveloping the earth as if to cradle it. Beneath this, a pair of hands held the Earth, as if nurturing, caring and loving this planet. The image then became blurred within my mind but not disappearing altogether. At this point two colors (and frequencies) covered the planet, as if it was clothed in a black and white patchwork quilt. It was as if a chequered layer of wrapping paper had sealed its beauty within it.

My vision, my 'self' and my very being seemed to drift into clouds of mist. I felt that many beings of light were gathering around me, looking after me, watching over me. These clouds began to drift apart and open. In front of me seemed to be a crystal clear pool of water yet it in reality it was not. For in the center was our globe and I realized (somehow I just knew) that this was being viewed from another dimension and we were all looking down upon it.

As I observed this, such sadness and despair encroached upon the feeling of peace that had previously enveloped me. It was an awakening to what was happening to humankind and their lives and to this beautiful planet. Yet strangely, there was a sensation of overwhelming power and a presence and energy bringing peace of mind to me. It started to grow even stronger.

Suddenly, a pink rose with its soft and elegant petals fell upon the 'water' and onto its clear stillness. Gradually, it submerged falling and spiraling downwards, with my mind, my consciousness following it. The rose began to shed its petals and these became sparkles of brilliant light, which contained love, life and beauty. They slowly started to sink further down the earth, into those white areas enveloping it. (I knew that this event, this gift of strength and of love was given to the light residing right here on this physical plane of vibration). My mind then became hazy and my consciousness blurred ... and I knew my experience had come to an end. Here are two pictures, which I hope will convey what I felt inside my heart. (PICTURE EIGHT: DIVINE LOVE TO ERASE DARKNESS AND HATE and PICTURE NINE: LOVE FROM THE DIVINE).

PICTURE EIGHT: 'DIVINE LOVE TO ERASE DARKNESS AND HATE'

Colors

PICTURE NINE: LOVE FROM THE DIVINE

I knew at this point I had to pick up the pen again. Dear friends, dear family of love and light, I miss you so much and am sorry my life has been busy and complicated not to be able to sit with you as often as I would like.

Please let your love and truth flow through me to conclude today with Violet (?) as I feel that 'Colors', Chapter Four is now drawing to a close.

COMMUNICATION: *We are here my son. We feel the connection of love to you and the entire world, together with the tingling of our energy through and over you. Remember that 'time' is only a fragment of your imagination and you say you are sorry for not being able to sit and hold this pen, but David, this is all right. Of those people who have said you need to understand and comprehend what you are doing, we state just be yourself, be 'you'.*

Trust is sometimes difficult, and we realize this. We do not (and never will) force you to pick up the pen, this will always be up to you. No malice, no force, no pressure, only our love and light. Others may question us while others may decide to ignore us. Some, because they do not understand us will try to say we are beneath or below a 'level' of intellect or wisdom they perceive exists or twists around them.

Let us explain once again ... we are no better or worse than any one of you in terms of who or what we are for we are all part of the creator. Yes, different vibrations of light and consistencies of 'form' but can anyone say we are unjust or should be below any one of you.

Someone who digests these 'works' (books) and concludes we are better than you, or show hatred towards you, or wish to manipulate you in any way, shape or form then we will be the first to accept and acknowledge that fact. We would then have to face our own karma and consequences from the love and light's true source–our God, your God. Please understand this.

David, when you became still and opened your heart and mind today, many feelings and images and a realization came to you. A sadness of hearts was felt. This is true only because we see what is happening in and around your earth-plane. The darkness and sin are trying to expand. A spiraling escalation of hate is over many places across your world, right down to the malicious damage in the material plane. (We knew your car tires would be slashed *[43]* and of the inconvenience and ill feelings it caused too.)

We say, do not be dismayed my son (and you all too) as the negativity can and does get drawn to many of your lives, your individual 'worlds' and families. As your frequency gets stronger it can sometimes attract those negative and dull vibrations to pick at, or attack you. Could these be lessons or even a balancing of your karma?

Overcome the annoyance and any anger, for it will be food and strength for those negative elements and forces around you. Let go and forgive (not always easy we know) and continue with your feelings of love. In prayer, pray for protection and for healing for all, as you well know Archangel Michael and his beautiful legions of 'Blue' (Angels) will come to seal, heal and also protect you.

ARCHANGEL MICHAEL

Archangel Michael and his sword of blue,
Keeping you safe right through and through.
The 'Light' and his all-blue lightning ray,
Both save and heal you night and day.

Yes, the full power connection from the creator's sword is beckoned through him to defend the righteous and all those who stand and wish to defend the love and the light. However, only by you and the many, can humankind's mass karma be diminished and dissolved leaving you free to be in eternal love. It is down to the individual to make that call and also make peace with God. (N.B.: We are digressing from 'COLORS' for these few pages to emphasize this important issue.)

We do not wish to judge you, but find it astonishing, so incomprehensible that the many take everything for granted and for what has been given to you. You are supplied with the air that you breathe, food to nourish the body, sunlight, water, and all that is required to sustain your very soul and being. Yet, there are many people that simply live for 'fun'. Being joyful in spirit is not the same!

Deliverance of Love, Light and Truth

There will often be no contemplation and thought regarding the negative effects caused by television, alcohol, drugs and hate and it can be the incorrect use of your senses and of your feelings to date. All these things can contain lower vibrations in their misuse and abuse and from overindulgence.

David, earlier today you saw the rose, the beautiful flower bud that fell into space and onto the earth. Please know that it was given as a helping hand to bring peace, love and bliss. It will increase the awareness needed to help raise the vibrations and bring color to these areas required to overcome the darkness. Each fragment of each petal is carrying a message to someone, somewhere striking a cord in a heart that needs a lift ... to strive forward with the banner of God's love. David, you now ask in your mind, 'Where did this rose, these beautiful 'symbols' come from?' I also hear you think, 'Why did it not float, just sink?

You need to understand you had witnessed this from a very distant place, the 5th Dimension. Yet this is just another layer, another vibration and frequency of time and space, where both the Ascended Masters and those from the higher octaves reside to flow and release their love.

Please know the rose you saw had a different colored 'core' ... one you could not see but need to feel for something more. The core and its color were pure VIOLET [44] my son and it carried the frequency and vibration that merges with all things. Yes, indeed the flame of Violet Fire to blaze away all hate and desire.

It fell and passed through each 'time' and 'dimension' to rest upon each individual in the separate countries and the designated nations. Was this an indiscriminate action or previously conceived? Of course, as in all things, light opens and closes as it is required and needed to be. Thus, strength and wisdom are guided to those who need it and who are in the right stage of their development with the raising of their vibration level.

Imagine a doorway in front of you and you consider turning the handle, will the door open wide or remain locked? The answer is clear, you cannot know this until you try!

The door will never open until the individual has tried it for themselves, and those that do must come to the door with love in their hearts. If this is the case, the door will always open as Jesus said, *"I AM THE OPEN DOOR THAT NO MAN CAN SHUT."* This remains true today just as it did the very first time it was relayed to the masses on the physical plane of your existence. David, you feel sad for a moment. Please explain why?

Its just that with such loving words around me I find it so hard to understand why there are so much hatred and misuse of the free will that God has given us all.

COMMUNICATION: *David, it's okay, we know how you feel. We know this is difficult, because on one hand we are saying you must try to cultivate yourself first (and all that is you), yet you also wish to try to change the world. Is this impossible?*
We feel you must look after yourself, your family and all that you are first David. Then linking your light with others will enable you to change things on a much larger scale. Eventually globally and universally, but only when enough love being emanated from all who live in truth.
Be never afraid my son. You will only be able to achieve what you have been empowered to do. This is why we say to listen to your higher-self and the Ascending Masters. Call for help from the eternal power of love that we have explained to you many times. Hm, we receive your thoughts just then too, and someone may well ask, 'Why doesn't God simply dissolve hate in an instant?'
As previously stated, the creator has never interfered but gifted the power of free will, but this has been misused over the millennium. It is now down to you all to use that free-will to break free and become permanently 'one'. Is it too late before the hate and darkness manifest themselves into destructive oblivion? It can be done by living the love, truth and light and by expanding the 'Violet Flame' and by living in peace and goodwill, yes indeed by living in Gods name. What we say might be depressing for some yet also very uplifting for many others. Again this depends on how it is received 'within'.
Okay, we will now finally conclude this chapter and the Violet and its 'hue'. So, what does Violet really mean to you? Well,

Deliverance of Love, Light and Truth

Violet, resonates and acts like a transformer. It releases and brings about change.

We know that many have discussed and deliberated upon the color and vibration of Violet and its wonderful splendor. It both radiates and spirals vertically and emits its beauty near and far, like a never-ending frequency of sound, a vibration of both forgiveness and of love. It can transcend and link your psychic awareness and other spiritual gifts.

It beckons you to open up, for you to receive and to give. It also transmutes that which is false both within and out. Know its frequency dances both below as it does above, for there is no difference, it is always the same, as it is made from pure love.

Try to visualize the Violet Flame dissolving all the imperfections of the 'bodies' you possess, and it will enable you to do so forever so that you can return to the one true 'Heavenly' body. Violet can bring this change and can take and clear away pain. It also lets love in to fall over you like you were in a shower of beautiful rain. Try to understand its frequency is again unique and never weak. It flows even stronger with the beckoning of your call to both the individual and also to the many, yes indeed it's the for the one and the 'one for all'.

If you dress in the color Violet, your awareness will increase and be more positive which will help to elevate all your cares. Know you are part of the all, so try to listen to your heart and soul which is opening towards the love and light ... and only to Gods call.

Once upon a time there was a coat of many colors. What will you (the individual) wear and think and feel today. Remember the words David that were spoken by Jesus when you were held in the light? "IF YOU FEEL WHAT YOU DO AND DO WHAT YOU FEEL, THEN ALL YOUR DREAMS ... WILL COME TRUE".

It is time for a little rest David. We have felt your heart miss a few beats recently with the decisions you are making financially and for your worldly cares. Re-read the last few lines. 'Feel what you do and do what you feel'. Let yourself flow with the changes taking place and you will find things will get better and you'll be in the right place to make other choices and decisions in the correct way.

In love and light please trust. Do your best, for no one can ask for more ... other than, 'What is the current balance of your karmic slate and score?' David let the pen flow once again when you are ready. Goodbye from us all.

Thank you from my heart for lifting up my heart as always. Goodbye for now to the pen, until my hand, becomes 'ours' once more again.

CHAPTER FIVE: LIGHT

Sunday 28th July 1996 (5.15 pm)

Dear friends and family of love and peace, I have missed your words of comfort both day and by night. As I open my soul, my heart, and my mind to the light, I feel I am protected and loved by 'beings' of truth oh so bright.

Dear Trans-leátions, you lift my heart and you shine and glitter brighter than any mineral, silver or gold. I love to hear your words and messages of guidance and hope ... and wish many others can learn from you rather than turning to the lower mind, the alcohol, or the 'dope'.

I realize people will do what they feel they have to do in life but I overwhelmingly desire they will all be able to experience what you have revealed to me in my life. So, as I now close my eyes, I pray you for you to hear my plea and call. Please send the words through this pen from another dimension, from love, from God and from Heaven.

COMMUNICATION: *My son, we are here waiting for you. As your mind, your consciousness comes across like a flashing beacon signaling over time, space and dimensions we can see, feel and also hear your thoughts. Therefore, we return with words of love for you all and hope these send the many of you yearning indeed for God's love and His true Heaven.*

David, earlier today you felt sad and alone as you drove home, yet deep inside you know you are not. Even when you think you are, we're actually together as you drive in your car. We felt your call and it touched us deep within, a pull of your hearts tender, loving string. (A soul's umbilical 'silver/crystal' cord.) So, lift your heart we say and continue this pen's journey, until the never-ending 'stay'. Is this another riddle or two? No, just to comprehend and to also do. Simply act and think without a blink of an eye, as missing out may make you cry.

Everything is as it should be at the current time so do not be concerned too much with not being able to achieve the things you wish to. Your needs will be met, as in the course of things, so no need to make a song or dance or racket and din. These are simple meanings when all said and done, so go forward don't dwindle, just simply move on. Just look for the strength for it's within all, just wish for it and want it then you'll hear the call.

We sense these inner battles within your mind, David. They sometimes rage on about the wrong and the right of life in and around the human race. As this was discussed in PATHWAY you understand you can only tend and nurture your own 'garden' and life first as others will link together and learn when they are ready to and not before. You are acknowledging the desire to succeed and to turn away from disease and greed, but people will only reunite when their hearts are open and stretch their arms out wide to embrace 'love'. An acceptance and learning both within and out will then lead to the comprehension of what they are and of what God, 'our creator' is all about.

Okay, today's communication will now include the start of chapter Five. This is important for those who have grasped what each color and vibration was, is and l always be part of. They will also understand they are different yet are also part of the 'same source'.

This chapter is called 'LIGHT ... and this is much more than a single word or 'name'. Thoughts may flash across your mind's creativity screen, but we will explain and develop this theme of what we mean. This information today will also be given with much rhyme and reason as 'light' is for everyone, every living thing and for each and every season.

So, what do we mean by a name? More importantly, what does a name mean to you? Perhaps it is a way of identifying someone or something? This may not be tangible but either way, this does not matter for a link or tag associates your thought waves and patterns of

Light

consciousness to identify and know who or what it is.

If we ask you what does the word 'light' signify to you, you might express it or try to explain it in various ways. You might describe it with another single word or with a picture, or by miming a symbol or even by pointing to the Sun or a star so far away. Is this childish? 'We are not kids' we sometimes sense and hear! Well, perhaps we all need to think like an innocent child once in a while to appreciate what we all are, and also what drives us a 'universal' engine deep 'within'.

Light is a simple word with five letters and could suggest one or two things ... brightness or weight? Are these connected or unconnected? You know the answer inside. The light we now speak of requires to be understood for across billions of galaxies, time frames and between 'planes' of existence and dimensions too, a realization will come that it is within and is you. This is because you are the creator, and the creator is you!

However, even though we explain this to you now, you may still feel that 'light' means the opposite to the darkness on the earth-plane or heavy. Please do not misconstrue or take in vain its real and true meaning, explained this day.

What if your soul was ignited like a spark from the almighty light? Comprehend a universal power resides in everything that exists. From matter to anti-matter, from molecular structures to the very space and time infrastructure that is linked to the creator, there lies the infinite love, which emanates from its core. Yes, the creator's heart can be said to be pure 'light'. How could anyone or anything really describe it, for the beauty and love is incomprehensible? So, where does this lead us now?

What we now move on to regards the knowledge accumulated across the millennium in many segments of evolution and from dimensions of time and space. However, 'time' as we have said many times before is only structured in your world the way it is to support the process of one's physical embodiment.

It is not necessary for other worlds to live as you do by the hands of a clock. Those who have opened the creators 'door' have turned the key of light in their own hearts, to find love and peace that for far too long has remained hidden but is now unlocked. Through tears

Deliverance of Love, Light and Truth

of hate and darkness and of sin and via your incarnations you must bear it all now to 'win'. Undergo a previously misunderstood task to now learn and to live right, to finally accept and understand the universal 'Christ' light.

We are going to open your minds a little further now, for across three of your solar systems lays a hidden Star. It resembles your Earth but remains dark. So far its light remains extinguished (as it has so long ago), compared to your planet which is like a precious jewel. The earth is part of a heavenly crown of light that glows and grows and is such a wonderful sight indeed both above and below.

Why do we mention this? Well, with your love you share and expel you can preserve and cleanse it ... for it can remain a place where you and other 'beings' from different galaxies and dimensions can go. Only by understanding the light can fade can you then appreciate that the previous star is now a deep black jade. It was once full of similar 'life' but has now ended forever. It's lying motionless, resting like the cold stillness of the darkest night.

Please know a hand of light is outstretched for you to grasp and understand what prevents you from knowing yourself. Do not be afraid of what others feel or think or say for it is your life to lead, to live and to play. In addition, please do not be angry or even shake your fist at those who love you too, but become connected to the strength that sustains you. As the light flows through you and your very core you will then crave and want and wish for so much more.

True love is infectious and as the light is love then the light will grow and increase in vibration creating peace and harmony in your lives and also for those who are close by you too. You can then shake the hands of your friends, family or neighbor and know that within them all is the universal Father/Mother God. Yes, each soul are born as 'light' from a source of true love, not a physical figure, a parent, a husband and a wife.

Therefore, everyone is a child of light and within you all resides the responsibility for the individual to shine so bright. Therefore, link your arms, your hearts and your minds and try to comprehend what has really made you.

Light

David, here is a scene, an image for you now to 'see'. Please try to describe it to thee.

Wow! I am experiencing a rushing sensation. Such speed, now my vision blurred, yet I know I am zooming through space to a very distant place. I now become aware of 'black holes' and of travel, of the incredible ability to somehow use these and why you do too.

Beyond such time and space differentials there is a planet, about the size of Jupiter ... with an 'inner' core which has belts of color around it. Beautiful and amazing, it resembles a gyroscope with a center of yellow and orange whilst the rings and belts are blue, red, dark orange and green. (PICTURE TEN: 'A BLACK HOLE TO DISCOVER THE GOAL'). Suddenly everything was blurred again ... unfocused as the rushing sensation returned. I then found myself strangely, back again!

COMMUNICATION: *Okay David, you have now seen this new distant planet, and we know people may say to you, "You cannot prove it exists or its location to us!" This is true David, but you do not need to.*

The reason why you know it is there is to show you the diversity of the light and its creation by the divine light source, the creator and of what God can create through love and energy.

There is no limit and no end. Everything is infinite in what the light was, is and forever shall be. Travel through galaxies and beyond is possible and you will also realize that what lies 'beyond' is also there within you wherever you go. It is also in every form of life.

On the earth-plane people will sometimes describe a 'discovery' by saying, "It is a new experience and therefore new understanding." What we are relaying to you is that all things are already inside you. If you are prepared to live your life in love and light and to achieve Ascension, then everything that was, is and ever shall be will truly be yours for all eternity.

It is now time to close David. When you are next able to sit (and be still), we will describe other places to you as well as other life 'forms' and how they perceive the light and the creator in comparison with yourselves. Interested?

We hope so, for as we said within the first few pages of this book, new information is being decreed through our connection of light from the creator to us, so that humankind may know more than you have ever, ever perceived before.

This does not make us better than anyone else. It is only from what our experiences and travels have gained and in what have been asked of us to share of the universe at this time. As we have said once before, the truth is out there, but it is 'within' and always was first. Goodbye for now.

Bless you, all. Thank you from my heart for your love and guidance today.

Light

PICTURE TEN: 'A BLACK HOLE TO DISCOVER THE GOAL'

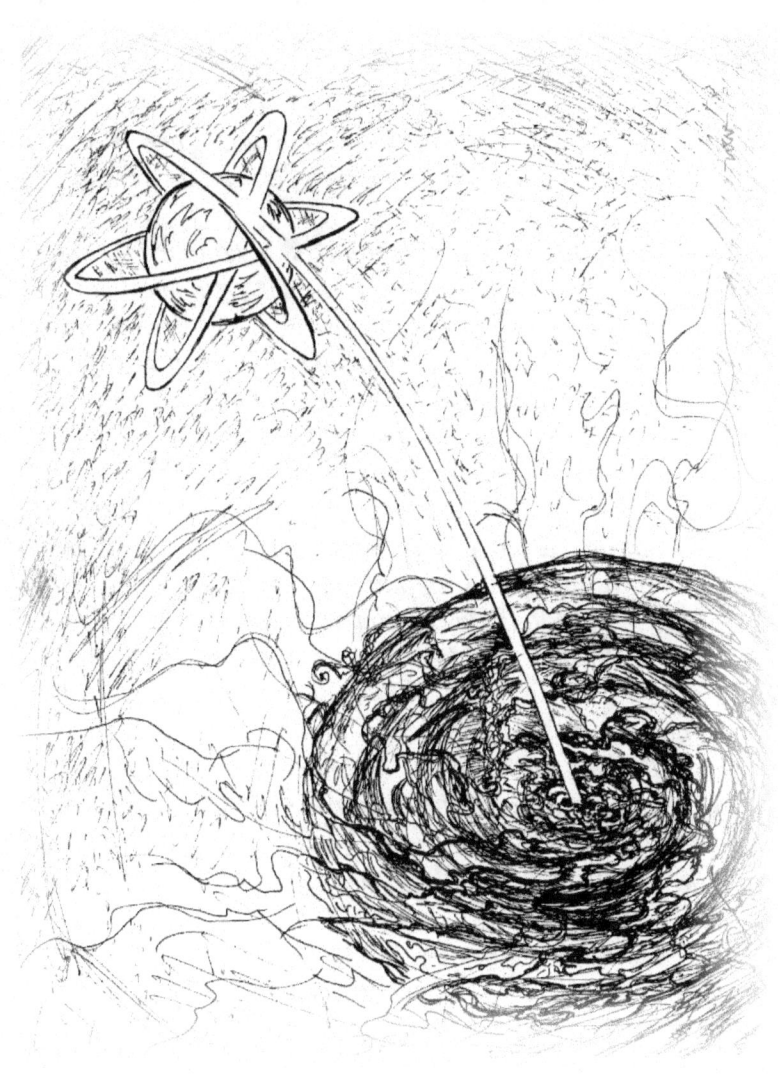

Friday 9th August 1996 (12.55 pm)

Dear Trans-leátions, you have been in my thoughts and prayers. Please now hear my call for new information for all. In love and light and truth...

COMMUNICATION: *We are here my son and have waited for you. We will always be ready for you. We hear your thoughts and connect our cord of light to you and your soul, which endeavours to shine for all to see.*

We have much to discuss with you this day and for the pen to flow in its usual way. There are many who wish to know of the love and light and they will soon discover there will always be so much more, as you can never stop learning in any way, shape or form. (But what does humankind consider to be the 'norm?')

Okay, we will begin today to pave the way for opening more hearts and minds, to crack open every hardened shell so that many more can kiss and tell. So, let's start with a recent event in your (Earth's) scientific discovery of 'life' [45]. We were aware that this was going to happen so the masses could query and continue to search for the truth. Please know that this will continue to go on.

We have both seen and heard many theories of the microscopic evidence (and existence) that fell to earth and which has been cracked open to be analyzed over and over again. Have we not recently said there are pieces of evidence awaiting discovery and the knowledge to be digested for 'progress'? (N.B.: We know that the 'rock' from Mars was not just found yesterday but the revelation and information of such which flew around your globe confirms our earlier message does it not?)

Your scientists have already gone over this, and we do not feel it is appropriate to reiterate it here. However, the events that have been shared (via various sources of earthly communication) are good because it means the 'average' person can also discuss and consider the information and 'evidence' for themselves.

So, is there 'life' on Mars? Of course! Life is everywhere, because the creator is everywhere. Though do no perceive all life as intelligent or to have evolved. Just as humankind has grown (this time around to this level of progress), so have millions of other 'beings' across billions of galaxies in their own ways too.

It does not matter that 'life' can be chemical or biological in structure or is different to you in shape or form. This is only a perception, for in fact all life comes from the power of love and light, and it is this one universal mixture that causes life and develops it in every plane and dimension of existence.

Humankind seeks more evidence and asks, "Could more evolved 'life' have ever lived there?" Know that Mars, (your 'red' planet) with gullies so deep and ridges and peaks so high, has secrets that will only truly be seen from within. We can hear those who will cry out, "So how can we prove this?" We urge those to seek inside their hearts for the answers.

We ask the world's scientists to continue to strive and test and search, but we also observe the scientific programs being set to send your technology further from the Earth. Billions of your different currencies across your globe are being spent to find 'life' out there. In reality everything can be seen 'inside' ... with no extra cost and no hardware!

Through the process and striving to learn all can make mistakes, but we should never blame another person or living thing for our own failures. It is only your will to succeed that will enable you to live and progress in real truth without hate and greed.

Know that life began on Mars very differently from planet earth, and in fact, it has been said it was an experimental planet. You could question this as the creator never makes a mistake. So how can this be so? Again we can reply, who benefits from this evidence now? Please think carefully about this.

Mars once had many rivers flowing with water and nourished valleys so serene, but it evolved to 'dye' red and not a living green. Gravitational forces and the elements in space wiped out the 'life' in an earthly sense, but there are still those important ingredients of light and love we have spoken about that are always there.

Therefore yes, life is upon Mars and your scientists will prove this. Eventually, there will be a day you will all perceive that energy exists everywhere, in every Star and planet both near and afar. Only current perceptions clouds these issues, so break away from the traditional thoughts and so called blinded visions.

For a moment we would like to continue the theme of the 'out there'. We know you are going to see a film at the local cinema David ... Independence Day. A sci-fi movie which has a restricted viewpoint and can control the minds of many. We state intelligent life is all around you. Do the masses think they are as yet, 'unfound?'(In a moment, a poem will come through on this matter).

David, please go to see the film, but please take it with a pinch of salt. Yes, an old-fashioned saying, but we know it is not your fault. Some may feel that what has been written today is speculation, for it gives no facts ... just imagination? In reply we say, come forth and feel from your hearts and deep within, give yourselves a start. Even when some information and proof of some kind is in front of you, in black and white, there is the tendency to disbelieve. Is this because they do not even believe in themselves?

The time is here and now to fulfill your true potential and goal to help yourself (and others) and to serve, using free will in God's name. Each of you may have a different road to embark upon and around each corner a new experience, a new task or test. Do not strive to be better than your neighbor, but enjoy (as you go through life) to move onto your eternal rest.

'KNOWN AND FOUND'

To be attacked in any way ... never will take place,
Ask, 'Why not by now?' ... if it really was the case.
And would fear then make you cry, to bring tears across your face,
Knowing your not alone, the earth and human race?

Civilizations across vast space ... they know that you are here,
But they do not have the right, to travel and interfere.
So, to condemn in any way, in shape or also form,
Would never be allowed, to be split or to be torn.

The intervention of the light, and the love it then endows,

Light

Dispels the darkness and the sin, from the one and from the crowds.
But interference from mere words, can both twist and be distorted,
Just as God's love and, light and truth, can also be transported.

If you endeavor to be kind, in thought and word and deed,
The pathway of your soul can flower from its seed.
Then be cast on 'winds' of change, for forever and all time,
To 'ascend' into the light, it is your right to be divine.

When you are knocked down by certain events, those which test your faith and seemingly push aside your own confirmation and evidence, just continue to pray for the truth. It is within you and it listens to you all, each and every day.

Those who can cope and have a stronger (not better) conviction, please help those who struggle and feel that life and their lives have been impaled. Can't go on? Is there nowhere to turn? Open your heart and let truth and peace, our God, our creator 'rain' in.

Truly, the light is so beautiful and bright, for it is never-ending and it has and holds no barriers in sight. It is a beacon of an eternal flame, which lies within you all ... never to part or fade or go cold and of course, is beyond any comparison with your so-called precious gold. Do not just listen to us and please, do not ever feel you are being told, for your very existence is yours to lead and you <u>can</u> break free from this karma and earthly hold.

David, it is time for you to complete the rest of your day's tasks now. Thank you for letting this flow today. We are always here for you, as you know. Goodbye for now as we send love and light and peace and truth forever to you all. P.S. For those who wish to hear, have no ego, and never ever fear.

Thank you, my dear friends and family of love and light. I wish to send my love to all of creation, every day, and every night. Bless you all.

Friday 23rd August 1996 (5.15 pm)

It has been two weeks since I have last picked up this pen. It seems so long ago that I have spoken to you, my family, and my friends. Please draw close to thee I pray; please hear my thoughts as I open my heart today.

COMMUNICATION: *We are here my son, just as soon as you had wished us to be. Your thoughts and wishes were carried across the lines of communication like a computer network, dividing pulses of energy and life, as if switching on a simple (and true) light.*

You also see a flame, for there is a fire within that burns with love. It fills your heart now and also forever fulfills your desire. We have waited and will always return to you and your thoughts when you need more of the love, light, and the truth. At each day and every step upon every road that you take in your life, we will be there with you.

Today, we will now continue and conclude this chapter Five of 'Light'. To describe things that will amaze your mind, and we hope to open the closed hearts of many of your 'humankind'. Just as we have said before, these new forms of learning will continue, like a search deep 'within' or perhaps some will simply find themselves, (their true selves) able to then cast aside any sin.

There could be a reliving of memories or for the individual to recall a brilliant glowing ember of light that for far too long has been hidden. The darkness of hate and superstition has lead to many people being suppressed, either by certain individuals or the masses or by authority or centuries of 'old' religions.

We have heard and watched you share your love and information and have stirred the feelings within those who have passed by to listen and reflect. Perhaps helping them to embark their own journeys now their spark has been reignited to shed light on their previously comfortable nest.

This is no deriding statement but aims to explain that perhaps they can now stand from their seats of rest and walk to the light upon the creators enchanted pavement and pathway. Walk to Heaven and far beyond the stars where no physical or material energy is required such as your earth's aeroplanes or cars!

A simple acknowledgment of what is really true, yes the light and the love is always through and through. (Then a new beginning will carry each one of you too). We know the Ascension has begun for so many of you now. It occurs both far and wide across cities and lands to touch your family and friends who are both known and unknown with outstretched hands. This forms a link, a joining and unification of each strand and these beacons of love and light that emanate from within and above and all around you will then be seen because the truth in people's hearts is starting to be found.

You pray, and these prayers together with your decrees and mantras of love and forgiveness are needed for the momentum to be maintained. Indeed, this will then expand the light to move further and further in all directions until the time is right for you all to leave and embark towards the creator's new home, a very real and promised 'land'.

In book one, Pathway, we had spoken of other dimensions and 'beings' who wait to unite and be free from the seemingly never-ending cycle of rebirth ... of 'life and death'. Millions of them across every galaxy and dimensions are preparing in their own individual ways. Each is continuing in their journey to succeed and return 'home'. Yes, from their seed of their birth to their fulfillment in coming to the new home (within the creators heart) being created and manifested at this very moment as we speak to you through this pen.

We know you sometimes have doubts my son about your own destiny, even after all you have been through. However, this should not make you feel you are wrong and it never will. The same applies to each and every one of you during your own search and goals and to know you will never give up.

Likewise, when you feel the ultimate goal of God's love is so far away you must withdraw from your conclusions because with an open mind you soon comprehend the creator is within you anyway! (And always will be.) One may realize this through a touch of hands or a friendly smile or even a beautiful scene, like the open land or sea or the wind that lifts the beautiful dove high into the sky. All represent the fabric of creation and as such, there is no need to ask the 'why'.

Deliverance of Love, Light and Truth

There is a place far beyond your galaxy and across many of your solar systems where there are beings who live simple lives, whilst other's are complicated and are sometimes beyond comprehension too. Perhaps it is time to take a look? Yes. Never before seen by earthly eyes or imprinted upon a mind but they can now be revealed for all humankind.

David, we will need you to place down your pen. Close your eyes, open your heart and be still. Know and understand you will be always be protected. May this new journey of your consciousness help you to understand and grow. You are linked into us so do not fear. When the time is right you will bear witness with your mind's eye, to enable others to expand beyond their own horizons too.

Be very still, for this journey of your inner self will touch your soul, to both see and help you to your eternal goal. Such fascination and so many new things to learn in the love and light inside your earthly home [46]. So for now, rest my son. Raise your consciousness above the mind. Slow your breathing rate down. Be at peace. No other thoughts ... just love and light to begin your journey and in great speed ... take flight.

Pause

COMMUNICATION (Cont.): *You are back now my son. Please now pick up your pen to write about your experience of what you have seen and done.*

As I write, I find it hard to keep awake. I am struggling to open my eyes and I feel as if I have been awakened from a deep sleep or am awakening from an anesthetic. Upon reflection, I also feel invigorated, refreshed and as if I have even been cleansed! (I will now describe what occurred)

At first, I did not know what to expect, or whether I had to wait to sense or feel something. After a while I seemed to be able to see through the roof of our home and up into the sky. Above me appeared the most wonderful brilliant light. It came closer and soon encompassed the whole house. Strangely, I seemed to be able to view this, as if from outside of myself, while also experiencing it at the same time too.

The roof seemed to totally disappear as if the light was now inside the house. Then came another light, in the form of a radiating beam or ray from within it. This shone down enveloping me. It beckoned me. It seemed to call to me, but without any words.

I felt myself being carried away within it, floating upward, up further still and into a spacecraft! (PICTURE ELEVEN: 'THE CRAFT'). It was as if my mind and my physical were together, yet also apart?

An immense rushing and tingling sensation overcame me. I sensed great speed, movement and travel and I knew instantly we had left the earth's atmosphere. I viewed the earth, but not with my eyes. It looked so amazingly beautiful and so serene, just like pictures and films on television or from space … Apollo 17.

Away 'we' went and through a 'hole' in space and 'time' were fragments of unknown light. A shifting or passing by, as if a million stars had glowed and faded into the distance. Suddenly, all stop. I know I was inside this ship or craft for I could see the Trans-leátions physically moving about. Strangely, it seemed as if their physical presence was for my benefit, for me to be able to observe them.

I could see some sort of control panel, it resembled a flight 'console' with an array of weird looking controls. Then I saw and recognized a special friend of mine … MILLANDERER! He came closer to me and it was as if he touched my hand. At this point I became completely surrounded and enveloped with an overwhelming feeling of love.

It felt as if I had a shield of protection placed over me. I sensed a layer of light, approximately 6 inches in depth, like an aura all around me. This was transmitted to me from his hand and his loving touch. (I felt this was needed to protect me, but from what?)

After this we moved through an opening to see through and out into 'space'. To the left of my line of vision, was an emerald green planet and it resembled an exquisite marble or pearl. It had four white areas upon it, which looked like polar ice caps, not only above but also to the left and right of its surface.

PICTURE ELEVEN: 'THE CRAFT'

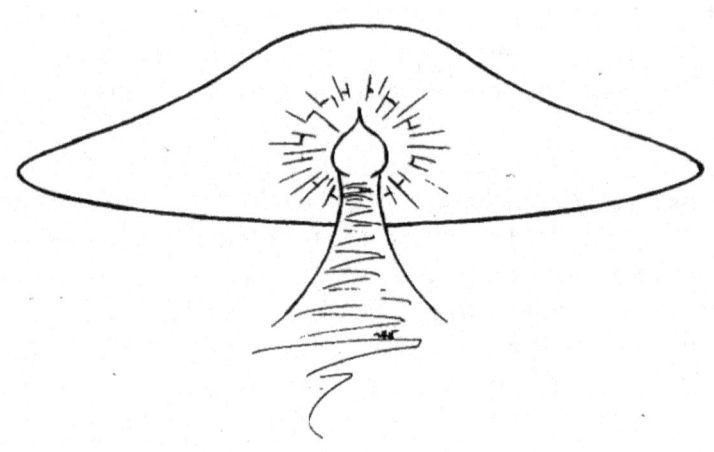

To my right was another planet, which appeared to look very similar to the earth. It was sparkling blue with a swirling mist, which seemed to partly cover it. (PICTURE TWELVE: 'TWO PLANETS').

My consciousness felt joined together with Millanderer's, as we seemed to be leaving the craft. We were being drawn towards the second planet and down onto its surface, to meet a new 'race' (not know to me) called the 'LEATURUS'. They were a species, a race of beings, which had developed spiritually in total peace with no wars or broken words of anger.

One of the Leaturus turned and seemed to gaze upon me. I knew instinctively that 'he' could read my mind, delving into my consciousness yet lovingly, peacefully without any forcefulness or pressure. He requested we should follow him.

I recall 'his' face and it resembled part human and part animal [47], as if elongated features of a dog or lion. Yet this seemed natural to me, quite normal in fact. It was as if I was able to accept this without fear or prejudice and was not even bizarre. In fact, complete normality, without a difference in feeling, talking and communicating with another human being.

His hair, which seemed more like a mane, parted at his ears (?). These looked like two pieces of large folded skin protruding upwards. The nasal and mouth area was slightly elongated while his face was covered with folds of skin, which overlapped smoothly. He turned and went to one side. This movement revealed he was wearing (what I would describe as) a cloak or habit, just like a monk would wear. I saw no legs or feet although that would suggest he was walking.

I followed him inside a beautifully lit cavern to a temple of some kind. In the center of this most peaceful place came a captivating and sparkling bright light, emanating from some object or altar. It appeared to have sloping shining walls, which seemed like it was some sort of support or stand. Above this was a huge circular disc, about 3 to 4 feet across its width, which seemed to shimmer and reflect like a mirror. On the outer edge of the disc were some sort of lettering or hieroglyphics of some kind. Perhaps it was a code or alphabet? (PICTURE THIRTEEN: 'LEATURUS AND THE TEMPLE').

I knew this was a very special gift that had been given to these beings by the creator. It helped sustain them and was also their means of travel for it was a 'portal' to many planes of dimension and existence. 'We' came out from the temple at this point and moved to view the horizon of this planet. What I saw were immense mountains and valleys as far as the eye and mind could see. The energy and vibrations of the different colors, in particular green seemed to fill my senses. There was water too, which was wonderfully clear and appeared as cobalt blue both near and afar. This was indeed an immensely peaceful and tranquil place.

Deliverance of Love, Light and Truth

PICTURE TWELVE: 'TWO PLANETS'

Light

PICTURE THIRTEEN: 'LEATURAS AND THE TEMPLE'

Suddenly it was time to go and return to the denseness of the body This felt like a goodbye, but only for now, as one day we would all be together as 'one' again. I understood, that they were waiting for this special moment and time too. Then there came an immense rushing, zooming sensation, which almost overwhelmed me as everything became blurred. Time and space began swirling around, yet strangely, it did not disorient me. For what seemed about a second, it felt I was not 'existing' as I would have perceived life to be.

Deliverance of Love, Light and Truth

Suddenly, I had been returned. A voice then said, *"Always look forward to the love and light and never look back."* It had been the precise moment I had tried to open my physical eyes. They were so heavy, but I must now pick up my pen. I now prepare to write again but also feel I must stop to reflect upon this most wonderful and amazing experience.

COMMUNICATION: *My son, you have been enveloped with my love as always and as a lending hand to 'see' new things. Please grow with the experience. Try to understand it through and with your heart. So, until the next time when your pen is ready, love and light to you all ... from us all. In God, the creator, always place your trust. Goodbye for now.*

May God bless you all and I send you love and light to you from deep inside me. As I sit and ponder and also recollect these experiences today, I know some people may perhaps read this and say, "You're having us on. How can we believe that!" I reply from the bottom of my heart that I would not and could not lie to you. I can only share my experience with you in truth and love.

This can be as real or false for you too. Is this my imagination or just a visualization? Are they all impossibilities or reality? I know your own heart will decide if you truly view these from 'within'. Until the pen writes again ... love and light to you all.

CHAPTER SIX: 'COLLATING DATA SINCE THE DAWN OF TIME'

I feel you all so close to me. I also sense the title of this new chapter seems apt ... so are we moving on from Chapter Five and the 'Light'? My heart is open and I send you my call, so please feel my love that is here for you all. Your son David.

COMMUNICATION: *You are right, and we are here to 'hear' you. Chapter Six will begin for the light has expanded and explained in different ways whenever required to do so within time, space and infrastructure of energy from the divine.*

So then, today can be new learning for a new beginning, or perhaps it will simply be a point where a change within someone's heart (from this additional information) can help others expand in other directions.

Information and data has been collated and imprinted into your very beings and souls and every structure of life since time immemorial. Indeed, ever since love and light has expanded from the creators' heart to install and start life in innumerable ways.

Like a computer or your human brain, information is imprinted, scanned, and digested and emitted into actions and thoughts. It is also within and upon every leaf and rock, every grain and molecule, every chemical, enzyme, or ingredient that can ever be known. The infrastructure of light contains wisdom, knowledge, love, peace, and the truth, so everything it contains can be revealed and expressed when the 'need' arises and also when the right time and circumstances are met. This principle remains across millions of galaxies and worlds and across billions of 'light years' to and for all life.

Deliverance of Love, Light and Truth

Likewise, across the dimensions of all existence of vibration and upon the immeasurable 'planes', both information and data is fixed, yet it is also flexible enough for a soul, a being of light to learn and grow and to change into what they require to be. (And in what they hope to achieve and to attain.)

What we mean by this is that as the individual soul passes onto a higher vibration and 'plane' then everything can be digested, learned and known through and within that level by becoming attuned to it, living it, becoming part of it by being it. This can be complex yet is simple too. Just as you are an individual being of light and living energy, you are also all 'one' because you are (as everything is) part of God ... a universal essence of the light within and out.

Understanding this is not difficult if you open up your heart. Let this sink into your very core and let it strike a chord within you so you can feel the hope and desire of the love it contains and sustains. (Everything will become clearer and easier for those who are not sure yet ... so then hopefully they will cast away the confusion which enveloped them before.)

Once your vibration and frequency (your resonance of light) has reached a sufficient level then the ability to learn also increases. Certain planes and dimensions can then be entered and visited to increase ones own inner awareness to a higher degree of spirituality, of love, light and truth.

There are though, many things on your earth-plane that remain static, for example, in the repetitive cycle of your seasons. However true learning will never stay this way. Your evolving soul can never stop growing, for a simple word spoken, a picture or scene viewed or photographed will always increase your thoughts and minds perception. Your lives never remain the same even though you often think or believe they do.

An elderly person in your community may notice something, for example, a small tree at the bottom of their garden and they gaze upon it every day and month. Then one day they believe that, 'it appears differently today'. Perhaps it is an overhanging branch or a piece of fallen fruit. Maybe a new shoot or a burst of colorful blossom, or they scent a sweet perfume that both drifts and lingers in the air.

Collating Data Since the Dawn of Time

They may close their eyes to think and feel; perhaps knowing that God genuinely cares. Yes, nothing remains the same, not here or there on the earth-plane or anywhere in existence. New growth is like this. A growing and learning and moving away from despair to when you leave your old 'self' behind you.

Let us look at the simple scenario of a fallen piece of fruit. Perhaps it is decayed and too bitter to taste, (so it is thrown away) not recycled, but gone to waste. A shame when we can recycle the life deep inside its core, to feed the land with its light, the light that you do not see anymore. This dead (?) fruit with it's shriveled and dried skin lies on the ground. It may be rotting away but the bacteria are life ... we shall and must say! By feeding and giving 'life' back to the earth (which is a living source for all humanity) it restarts the cycle of death and rebirth within all things.

This is the basic truth many already know. Though some may often need a reminder to feel this deep inside and not to just care about themselves. We do not imply that none of you cares or that you should all now go out and recycle every organic substance ... but ask you to re-affirm and understand the principles that were given to 'all' since the dawn of awakening. Many civilizations and planets with their different religions know and understand this while others have denied it or passed it by tossing the truth aside either by word of mouth or by sleight of hand.

Life is so precious in its many forms and perceptions and is so beautiful too. Life is love and it is no illusion. It is truth and it is of your physical body as well as 'within' and in all your lives. So, by having any hate within oneself then darkness will settle and at some point, can overwhelm the individual and their surroundings.

Know a physical body wracked by disease is caused by misuse of free will, both from the past and/or the present, together with the intoxication of its living cells. Stress equals disease too, for illness is never divided as it is all linked and never separated until love and light has entered in. (Remember, the physical, mental, emotional and etheric/astral bodies are four, yet also one.) Sometimes this physical side of you acknowledges the 'hate' and therefore this line and these words can now be learned, digested, and perhaps will help you to now to go on to debate?

Deliverance of Love, Light and Truth

Ask and then answer (yourself) a question in relation to this simple thought. If you have an argument, fight or quarrel, or even a misunderstanding with your father, mother, sister, brother (or perhaps it is with your wife, husband or even your lover), do you have or feel an ache inside you? Was it in the pit of your stomach and so strong that you can't digest? Do you feel sick? Have you gone all hot or cold? Why? Just try to understand these words and how the other person may also feel.

These feelings of pain or anger manifest in many ways and these leave traces of negativity within your life core and inner radiating coil. These twist and become misshapen into incorrect spirals, upsetting the functions of your mind, body and soul. Your chakra's then divide and rotate in separate ways, which then leads to self-decay..

Everything possesses information of the light, from the sentient being to the insect that crawls across the floor or ceiling. Remember too, even though a 'life' may not breathe, it does not mean you should give up upon it. Life is always lived in one form or another. It always exists as so.

In the next part of this chapter, we will discuss your earth and much more. We will let you know of some of the wonders of your earth, together with 'information' that emanates from its core. Know the land and seas and also the sky each carry life in so many ways, and we will be here to help you know the answers to the how and why of these. Please listen to your voice and inner self for this is the light, which is your light. Thank you from our hearts to you all. In love, light and peace, goodbye for now.

Bless you, for today as always. My love and light I give and also send to thee.

Saturday 14th September 1996 (3.00 pm)

I feel your connection drawing close to me now. It's strange how it seems such a long time ago. I am ready to let the pen flow from your heart once again. I hope that those who wish to seek and learn may know more of your love and light which pours through and over me, just like 'Heavens' rain.

COMMUNICATION: *We are here my son and have waited for you.*

A gathering has taken place on another 'plane' and dimension to watch and listen to. Please know what takes place is not just a single connection all of its own. You may think that as your pen is writing and the communication flowing, only one or two beings of light who are close by, but it is often many more than this. Yes indeed, there are the friends, family, teachers, and guides of many who look and listen today to feel the light that both emanates and shines so brightly.

Your recent meditation gave you renewed vigor and strength and with the love and light drawing close, you will gain and grow in the love from what is both said and also in what is shared through you. Love and light are universal and so what is given out also returns. You are well aware of this next line and what it means, 'So you sow and so shall you reap'.

Okay, let us move on now from where we had last left you, to discuss the world you live upon and its life 'core' and energies too. (This special place humankind resides upon and 'in').

The earth-plane and its structure have been studied by many of your scientists and philosophers over the centuries. They have made numerous breakthroughs of magnificent proportions. These have shaped and changed the way you have all lived as beings and souls on the physical 'plane'. Yet, as we have mentioned before, there are still major discoveries to be made both upon the land and sea but will these remain hidden? This we hope is a burning question that will lie inside the individual or the masses around the globe.

You also probe 'space' and the so-called 'unknown' yet only a handful of prominent people have asked or stated, 'but what about within?' In this particular instance we do not mean within your heart or mind or soul but inside your planets protective layer and 'skin'.

There are those who say they know all about the Earth and what lies inside the planet ... of what chemical deposition makes this or that and also what extinguishes another. However, the information that's truly required is simpler to be found when

Deliverance of Love, Light and Truth

looked for in the right direction and in the right place!

Today, we have been given the dispensation to relay to you from the light within us to say, 'go and seek and find the truth'. It lies in the past, but also resides deep beneath the intelligence of you ... in humankind. This is a clue, for both deep inside and also on an ocean floor lie more answers for those who want to know much more.

Many of you feel the earth's knowledge has all been revealed and its crust fully investigated but it is time to rethink this with both new technology and redevelop (externally and internally) with it. What will be found (when the time is right) we are not able to divulge but we know for sure a discovery one day in the ocean so blue will cause the world to think, 'Can this really be true?'

Mm, what can it be? What will be found? Is this a real or just an illusory sound? What we can tell you is that it will have a profound effect on every nation. Not because of what is actually there but because it is something for you all, the knowledge and wisdom gained are to be given out and shared.

We can also inform you this finding will come via a joint nation 'alliance' though we will not tell you of a 'time' for this event. Please do not say this is another 'opt-out', or that you have not given any exact facts again!' Let us restate the purpose of our existence and the task we had set upon before humankind even existed, which is to help and serve God, the Great Spirit, the creator in the 'love, light and truth'.

Do you question 'Him' for 'His' actions and the results of life and death and of evolution and existence? We can all ask questions this is true, but the truth is in knowing, trusting and having the faith, wisdom and the understanding to accept that certain things are done at different times of life (and existence) ... exactly when they are meant to be.

The Ascended Masters do ask and question, but they do not question the light 'within' for it is such an extremely high frequency they accept the resonance of truth. This should easily relate to you when you comprehend that certain events and occurrences are far more complex than a simple decision or by the simple answer of yes or no. You should not detract this from the fact

Collating Data Since the Dawn of Time

you can test those from the spirit world (or indeed any guide or teacher) in what you receive. Indeed, they often expect it if you are searching for the truth.

We know you would also like us to explain in which of the earth's oceans the discovery lies. This is not a joke or poking fun, for it would be easy for us to say. However, do you remember the scenario (in book one Pathway) of the child's first day at school? Living and learning is infinite and so, like the child, you all need to grow and also discover. Only when you are ready will you find out what is to be learned. It will fundamentally change the way the masses think and feel about each other and also about themselves 'inside'.

Perhaps at this point of your future then those walls of hatred that so many countries have erected will then be torn down to reveal the truth, and in turn, gateways will be open to the light. We will see and you will then understand. Therefore, look to the depths of the oceans for there lies an answer so strong and wonderful it will light up your hearts and minds and your voices to sing and sing!

Okay, now let us move on again. Both within and around your planet lay a multitude of networks of energy and these are linked together like a 'spaghetti junction'. Like your many roads, they lead to certain destinations. Upon your earth-plane, you travel your own road and can sometimes get lost or stranded (so you think), but you can also keep the knowledge on a soul level that you are in fact traveling on strands of beautiful love and light. Amongst these almost infinite vibrations lies a Pathway for an individual and the masses that will lead to your new home.

When the right connection and vibration is reached and the correct level of light has emanated from within, you can be relayed together with the exterior 'bands' of light (from the core energy throughout time and space) which mixes and interfaces across the universe. This enables the Ascension process to take place, and many beings and life-forms use these grids and connections of energy to travel across solar systems and galaxies from one place to another by the linking of frequency and vibration.

On earth, the connecting interface consists of seven points of energy collected and distributed at designated places. They can be described as universal 'generators' of immense proportions. You might ask, "Who was the engineer?" The answer of course is the creator! These seven places are known to many but are often contemplated very differently by them too. There is one in the America's, another in Great Britain, one in Asia, Egypt and India as well as at both the North and South poles. Some people (as we have said) already know this and it is part of their karma to help you all in this respect.

They know these are very special places and perhaps when they are there they feel something is alive within them. Perhaps something far, far greater than could be imagined? They know by being there or connecting with their hearts, minds and souls it makes them feel more alive than they already do. If you could see the energy and the power and love that radiates and encircles the globe from these, we know that you would weep with joy.

As discussed before, it is from these seven collection points that the 2nd, 3rd and 4th wave of Ascension will leave the earth-plane. Those souls on those waves do not physically have to be there but on the subtle level, they will know this is where they will first connect before interlinking with millions of other beings together in the new home on the plane of 'Community'.

So, the Earth is an incredibly special place. It is beautiful, and everyone should try to maintain its beauty and balance of life. This is why it is important to think and feel before you act with any darkness and or hate. Any anger or hatred that emanates is picked up by the 'elements' ... the life-forces within you and also on the land, and in the air, water and fire. Each is a composite of creation and each has their own job to do.

Appreciate they carry the negative energy that is given off by humanity but they cannot always maintain the balance or rightful state of harmony. This is so often why the earth explodes, hurricanes whirl, and fires rage and is what also causes both destruction and rebirth. These energies cannot and will not carry disharmony forever. They can also only cope with so much negativity that is given off by karmic imbalance from peoples heart's, souls and minds.

We know some people who read this will be able to relate to what we are saying, but others will still need to learn to understand at a later date. If they become still and open up to the love and light, this will then become easier to comprehend and then adjust their fate.

Through prayer, decrees and by simply helping each other the love and light will flourish and continue to grow sufficiently around and within you all. Therefore, by connecting the necessary fluxes of energy and life to those that already exist, their ascension can take place at the designated 'time' frame of their individual lives. (This time around in their present incarnation!)

Okay David, today is drawing to a close, and we hope what we have discussed creates more burning questions deep within. Just like the earth's molten core, which sometimes bursts through its outer surface to be released and heard again once more. Until the pen flows once again in love, light peace, and truth. Goodbye.

Bless you, from my heart. Love and light to you, from your friend who knows that 'he' is part of you.

Saturday 21st September 1996 (2.15 pm)

Hello to my teachers and guides. Please draw close as the pen is ready once again for your love and light. You are so far away yet so near to me that I feel an innocence, so sweet, just like a small child, who will never fear. Draw nearer than near and hear this plea from my heart.

COMMUNICATION: *We are here my son and connected to the truth to hear your plea from deep within thee. We have watched and seen your tears that flowed from your eyes, but in truth they have come from deep 'inside'. The meditation you have just been through lifted you up and kicked out any doubt. You recalled the messages from many, many moons ago and also remembered there's no need to scream or shout.*

We know of your feelings and decisions and the search for the truth ... and wondering of 'when'. (Your personal thoughts not to be openly shared, David.) Remember, have faith. It needs to be strong, for you and for others too. Also, there are those who will be relying upon you to tell your story and your experiences.

Deliverance of Love, Light and Truth

Yes indeed, so that you're own strength can be passed on for others to know and to grow too. This strength can sometimes hide, and the yearning can make you cry. Please be patient. It will come through for you, we promise.

You are going through a testing time. One that we have all gone through and each and every one who reads this can also probably relate to a particular problem they have as individuals, or within the family 'unit' at this moment of time. So be strong and maintain your trust within your heart. You will succeed and overcome the difficulties created by circumstance within or around you by your own karma or the karmic state of others.

Lift your heart to the love and light and you will always be okay. Well, now to press on and complete this last part of chapter Six. First of all we are going to tell you the way we collect information and how we can relay it to you and many other civilizations across the universe.

Consider what a computer and also your brain are capable of.. They feed and grow and learn. Some say they are 'programmed'. When humankind developed computers were they not huge machines, their memory very slow? This was no different to your own brain's thirst for knowledge, wisdom and also for understanding too. What limits have been placed on a computer chip or digital output? And likewise what limits does one set or give oneself as a person or soul? Is this now something too complicated or too difficult to comprehend? Let us enter a new program to speed up the process and enable the machine or robot to increase its productivity and output.

Your mind's connection is a link to the brain and your scientists and scholars have not explored this in too great a depth. It craves for knowledge and both expansion and expression and it will always continue to do so. Why? For this is inbuilt, within you. As the etheric, mental, emotional and physical bodies of the 'self' are connected so is the 'self' to the inner self. Is this now too hard to take or to swallow? Hm .... the microchip has been decreased in size in such a short space of time and it now undertakes more work. Yes, more movement and actions are sending pulses of energy and intellect in many different directions. It is this comparison, this link and this point of view that we are trying to 'relay' now far across to you.

First of all, this is to show you how we have grown and also for you to learn and expand in the same way if you can. By concentrating on your energies within and by expanding your mind and brain by multiple functions you will be connecting pulses of energy throughout your 'bodies'. Our light infrastructure is like a computer as it connects pulses of current and the energy which flows from point-to-point and place to place to try to lift hearts and minds and also bring a smile to many a face. We are not mechanical of course and never have been, but the multiple functions of your computer silicon chip or human brain is very similar even if only by name.

We connect to the power of the creator on strands of light (just as you do), but in a slightly different way. We are also like a computer, which also needs to feed on a power source. So, to function and grow and to be compatible, we need love and also for the ability to share our knowledge and wisdom to new 'terminals and screens'. Therefore, we can show how both the individual and the many can grow and also know what we mean.

People often say a computer is only as good as the information or knowledge that has been entered within it and this relates to what is also taken out or viewed or accepted! What nourishes us can also be given out to you and we only 'say' (as the proof is within your heart) that what we share is the truth, because we are fed and sustained by the light that 'is' or 'is part' of us all ... our God.

Within us is a matrix that functions in many ways. It is like a receiver and sender or transformer all in one. This is also like a 'heart' to us. These are very complex and the connections are of minute, almost invisible proportions. We suppose you could compare what we mean (in size) to the splitting of your 'atom' again and again for we know you could not see it, yet it exists. Like so many things though throughout the galaxies, many beings have said and thought, "If I cannot see it then it's not real" or "that it does not exist." Remember, it all depends on how you view it!

We would also like to say that your hearts are no less wonderful or beautiful and are an amazing creation in keeping our physical

Deliverance of Love, Light and Truth

bodies alive and well (normally). What you cannot see is the spectrum of light and love that emanates from within and also around your heart too.

This can also be described as a matrix and the invisible heart of 'color' that feeds your soul is like a pump. This enables the energy within your core to flow way above your stellar gateway chakra [48] and also below your feet and beyond your earth star chakra which connects and 'grounds' you and your energy levels.

Why do we talk of this today? Well this chapter is about collecting 'Data' so perhaps this information will be new, whereas, for others, there are some parts already known. We are also saying we are created from the same light but are different in structure as we are 'set' in light ... rather than with different frequencies as you are. You also have varying needs at this point of your growth.

This information has been given today as we are all connected. What is learned though can always be found directly inside you. It can be guided along though by others like us. It is our task from the creator but it will always be your individual choice to sip or quench your deep thirst that you may have.

Information is universal and as we have said before it comes from one 'source' and one source only ... the creator ... God. However, the knowledge and wisdom can be found in each leaf, rock and place, and I every time and dimension that has ever been 'created'.

Recently we have spoken of the Earth's core and also of 'hidden' knowledge...and now we will reveal some more. Connections of energy from the earth also flows up and through you like the computer matrix we had described earlier today. In a physical sense, it also contains much truth on its outer and inner layers and this is what we mean when we speak of 'collating data'.

It expresses itself because it is alive with light and love just like you and me. Therefore, it is important you are in tune with yourself so you can understand and feel the life force that radiates and emanates from it. Know these energies are part of what sustains you and your very being!

David, we are going to let you see and draw these layers of energy that are both within and around you and the Earth.

Collating Data Since the Dawn of Time

However, as a certain amount of this information ('re' chakra's for example) has already been discussed and passed on by others on your earth- plane, we wish you to draw a picture of the human heart surrounded by the life force that links with the soul instead. For a moment, please place your pen to one side. Now open your eyes of your heart and mind to truly see not hide.

Okay, please now describe what you have experienced.

At first, there was a rushing and tingling sensation over my entire body. Then, a strange feeling, as if a shifting or sliding movement within myself took place. Suddenly I became aware I was actually viewing 'inside' my heart! Veins and valves were like fibre optics as if seeing through keyhole surgery, from the end of a microscopic camera placed within me. (But in greater detail.)

Around my heart were pulses of light 'coils' radiating outwards like a beacon. As I viewed this, I knew instinctively the outer colors changed according to how we all felt, with our emotions, our health and upon our vibration level of light. The inner whiteness remained but it would become darker with decay and hate, or it would shine even more brightly when more love has entered in. (PICTURE FOURTEEN: 'THE RADIATING COIL AROUND YOUR HEART'.)

I then learned that upon Ascension of your soul, the 'White' turns to the color of Mother of Pearl, a soft hue and a beautiful glow that reveals the true you as you rise to live the eternal truth. Yes, this was such a wonderful feeling indeed. I thank you dear Trans-leátions for helping me to see and understand this too.

COMMUNICATION: *Okay David. Time is drawing near for you to relax and rest with the weekend to pause, reflect, and draw your breath. When you next sit, we will be ready with chapter Seven and we are calling this, 'A LIFE ... ALIVE.' We will explain why this is so when you are ready next time my son. Goodbye in peace.*

Thank you for your love and light that flows through this pen, for surely the Truth is only 'Heaven' sent.

PICTURE FOURTEEN: 'THE RADIATING COIL AROUND YOUR HEART'

CHAPTER SEVEN: 'A LIFE ... ALIVE'

Friday 4th October 1996 (7.00 pm)

Thank you for last night's dream and message for I now understand and know of what you mean. You were so far away in the depths of the night yet also so near that this pen may write. Please know I love you all and I thank you for your light and protection. I can feel the pressure building up around me as you draw so close ... bringing such peace and tranquility.

COMMUNICATION: *The cords of communication are as strong as ever my son and always believe in this. You may sometimes have doubts and feel steered away, too busy ... wrong timing, not today? Trust in your heart and let it flow and this pen of yours will always reveal the messages to be shown.*

We watch both from near and far as we have said many times before. The connection and link across time and space is from heart-to-heart. Nothing can break or deceive it and you feel and recognize us when we are close and this will always remain so. This evening David, there is much to say to you but also simple meanings that can and will be viewed only by those with an open-heart and mind too. We reiterate and state this because it is for the individual and for the masses when they are ready. It is not for us to say that everyone will read and understand this or that it is for only 'one'.

It is down to the truth and light overcoming the doubts of darkness in people's inner selves and their surroundings. This will happen in the appropriate 'places' when and where it is needed most, but it can (and always will) be expanded by the calls from a soul and the opening up as we continually state to you.

Deliverance of Love, Light and Truth

When someone's exterior shell is cracked open by another's helping hand or upon their own search for truth, then the light will flourish and will grow with words and actions of love. There will be no malice or condemnation. Believe and be believed is what will keep saying to the many and keep grounded while your work of love and light is to be done. (Not head or heart in the clouds, because this will be no good for you or anyone else either).

Balance and understanding is very much a seesaw thing, like a scale to be tipped over by the weight of someone's word or their thoughts bringing joy or those of hate, which brings both pain for their own gain. To obtain equilibrium you need to be still, to go within and touch the loving flame and lift your heart to sing. This can be an easy thing to do if you only just be you ... and are always being true.

Okay, now moving on. If we were to say to you that you could be alive, but also dead, would you understand? Could you comprehend? In general or in physical terms, you would say you are alive until your heart stops 'beating' i.e. are 'technically' dead. On your earth-plane, you of course may be right. In reality, though is the word you call 'dead' a meaning falsely placed inside your head? Many theories will of course be put forward on this.

Consider a victim of a car crash or child in a coma, or of someone who has had a 'near-death' experience of the golden light at the end of the tunnel. They describe an enveloping, nourishing love so immense they believe they have never known it before. The feeling is so strong they can recall this accurately upon waking up again. Perhaps becoming a changed person, who then lives life to the full? Enjoying its richness, and becoming a believer in love, light and in God and knowing that life is not for suffering from any illusory fever.

Some skeptics (and they have their right of opinion) may say this is caused by oxygen deprivation to the brain ... or that the brain is switching off before it soon decays. In addition, these people experiencing such events do not speak the truth and this is not reality.

We say it is them who cannot understand (but not to chastise them), so we encourage them to re-evaluate the theories of

A Life ... Alive

their scientific programs and for human kinds progress too. Do you have an opinion on this? Also, some will state, "You (and they) have no proof too." Yet we reply love and light is the truth and the individual receives their own proof in their hearts.

Understand by drifting toward the light and overwhelming love cannot and will not be able to be reproduced by any virtual reality machine or by self-induced cardiac arrest because true love cannot be put to these or any other sort of test. So, what should one do when their loved one lies 'asleep' on their back? Will they ever wake again? Will the families ever get back on track? Pray, please pray my friend, for this is what you can do and if a return to the earth-plane is meant to be then they will 'pull through.' Be not afraid of what you and they may face because if they cross over, then they will be returning 'home' to beyond the truth to an open Heaven's gate.

A life goes on living, even if you do not think of it as being ALIVE, for it always goes on to strive and strive. The soul grows to better itself and not to remain in the ground or to be turned just to dust. Although the pain of loss may never seem to go away the love you share will always also remain for it cannot be erased through time or space.

David, your mind forms a bridge to contemplate what we have just said. Please continue to let the pen flow and a poem may reveal what you wish to know. Feel what we have tried to say, reveal it now but perhaps in more than just one way. Think of us but never, ever forget to look (and feel) beyond the stars. We are here and always will be to send you all our love before we duly go. Do not shed a tear and be strong.

You will give and share this in other ways when the 'time' is right. 'Till then, in peace and love and light do trust. Do your best in what you say and do, as no more my son can be asked of you. Know that we love you all. Goodbye.

Thank you for such love and peace this day. The poem I will place right here, for I feel it will dispel many a heart that fears. It is incredibly beautiful. Thank you from my heart.

Deliverance of Love, Light and Truth

THE TUNNEL

The gentle beating of the heart will stop to soon decay,
While clenched fists try to punch 'restart' ... though soon are put away.
The stillness in the air now breaks with pain and fear and grief,
And even holding of your hand is soon to be released.
'NO!' screams out the cry and shriek from way down deep inside,
With shouting out so very loud, "Oh, please God tell me why?"

The soul departs a voyage again upon the one split-second,
And in love and truth there it's found, the doorway now to Heaven.
The darkness is then broken ... and shattered by light so bright,
Reflections in a mirrored glass, like beautiful rays of light.

A swirling pale white mist ... descends and envelopes your 'all',
When the 'inner' realization comes, of 'love and lights' true call.
Though friends and family come ... and then circle all around,
But they cannot see or hear you, or know you're safe and sound.

Those souls now sparkle brightly, as you drift and light envelops,
A most powerful sensation yet, now beckons and develops.
To lift and spiral you, 'above' the plane and new dimension,
Yes, dear friend it's true, beyond all doubt a life in Heaven.

There is no solid 'mass' at those so-called pearly gates,
But with energy, truth and love and the light that is your fate.
It is there for you today, and forever an eternity,
Your love entwined together, not to fall or leave a certainty.

Now upon those precious lips, falling tears that they have cried,
Of those who are so close, do not think the last goodbye.
We ask no longer fear, and know your love that's torn apart,
Will grow now even stronger, to mend your aching, broken heart.

Saturday 12th October 1996

I feel a little strange today. I guess I am a bit out of sorts, as if I am not really with it! Still, I hope and pray for love and light to connect with the truth and for what is right. Please … my friends and guides and teachers … dear Trans-leátions, please come to help and teach us.

COMMUNICATION: *David, we are here, but sense you feel a little in doubt today. Do not worry and do not be overly concerned or shout. Sometimes your mind is busy on other things and that is why the frequency can dwindle or change as we have explained to you before. Do you recall?*

Today we just have a poem for you to help you all understand. When we last communicated with you, we had spoken about the 'Tunnel of Love', well this poem is about the life 'Beyond', and yet it is still the life 'Alive'. A life that's totally free and eternal. It is simply called,

BEYOND

The heart of the physical, has beaten to a stop,
And the flow of blood will now … congeal into a clot,
It has paused within the veins, but is no longer in vain,
While the life force holds the truth … and is never one to blame.

You have spiraled once again, through the tunnel of bright light,
That lights up the soul's pathway, but is it day or is it night?
To know truth is not beyond, so you no longer do despair,
For your reality is the peace, within the creator's love and care.

A vision or a picture will reveal its own true self,
A mirage or an image, that you debate, 'Oh is that self?'
In truth, you will connect, to the 'inside' you to know,
That beauty lies beyond the barriers, you had erected all below.

It's time to now reflect, and that you are your own judge,

Deliverance of Love, Light and Truth

Your soul yearns life eternal and may never want to budge.
And as the Ascended Masters gather, in mists of love not smoke,
The elixir of love descends, one that gives you 'life' not choke.

Then pause on where and why, and on the things that you have done,
For you then must decide, are you part of the universal one?
Only inside and deep within, is the reality of your core,
To understand what you are, and of what you've been before?

The choices you will make ... as you discover then the truth,
Now consider all your actions or what you seek inside the proof.
You'll find it's all mapped out, been decided by soul and 'Source',
Embark on different journeys or stay upon this course.

In love and light and truth, are the decisions you will take,
They are yours of ones 'free will', and yours alone to make.
To return one day perhaps, to help others live and learn,
Or remain in light forever, not to cry or shout or yearn.

Only you will know, of what has to be done,
An acceptance thus so far, and the joining of the 'ONE'.
And why a tunnel stays wide open, in both directions you will see,
Recognition of the choice ... in love and light to 'be'.

David, bless you for the connection today, but the time is weak and today your frequencies low. Please rest and do the things you need to do. Then begin again when you can, to start afresh and to continue with the end of Chapter Seven. Remember we are always with you in peace and truth. Goodbye.

Please can you forgive me? I will be stronger and more ready when the pen next flows. Thank you from my heart.

Saturday 26th October 1996 (3.15 pm)

Please 'tune' into me, for I need your guidance more than ever. I need to feel your love within and around me and desire to share your knowledge and wisdom.

COMMUNICATION: *My son, a circle envelops, for there is a need to 'develop' and people will be drawn to you because of the need inside themselves and for their 'self' to grow and find. Be ready to hear their call for you will need to help them and as you do so in this new period, you will learn and develop too, together as 'one' as we all are and will always strive to become. Look with your eyes; your heart and your mind and certain events will be triggered and help all who come together to the light.*

These are busy times you are going through and they are frustrating too, but remember to turn within for that is your 'time' and no one else's. Your 'self' deserves this 'time' for expression and growth and how many times have you said this yourself! Do not let the outside world dictate to you too much, although of course there is work to be done and your needs to be met. However, find the right way that is best for you to see you through. Listen to 'within' and you will know when to let go, so you can continue to grow.

Know that peace and love always surround you and you will touch and feel this. The everlasting love and light never separate by day or night so when you need to, you can express and seal the love and protection 'in'. All you can ever require will then lead you away from any desire or sin.

Remember be yourself and not what anyone else thinks or wants you to be. It does not matter what material things are around you like what type of car you drive, because you proceed at the only true speed and motion that is for 'you' alone. Everyone must simply be themselves to express their true self. As long as this is done in the name of love and light ... and not to hate or kill or to fight!

Okay, let us move on, some words and pages to be fun. To complete chapter Seven and to move on again, or is there more perhaps, even eight, nine or ten? These will give you a structure to work to and for you to complete these works (this book) and then who knows where it will lead you next.

We know you are proud of what you have done and of what is taking place so come on David ... put that smile back upon your face. A happy 'you' means 'happy' through and through and you will rejoice soon, make no mistake of that. Some of your wishes and hopes are about to be realized and a little more patience is all that is needed. Just wait and see.

Okay, Chapter Seven to conclude so no longer to brood. We ended last time with a poem; did you think it was Heaven sent or was it just a mystery being described by one's pretense? Perhaps these messages or meanings are tools to power up the engine within oneself, or to drive forward the goal of acceptance, though we would never say you are being anybody else's fool.

Imagine for a moment that you have 'crossed over' through the tunnel of love and a realization has been understood. Is there a time constraint or pressure to achieve? Do you have to return or do you truly then believe? On this higher plane of vibration (a temporary home until the new 'plane of community' is completed) you will make new choices as your soul and soul's creation both connect to help you decide.

Then, you can go on to learn more on that plane or return to physical matter to serve or grow in other ways too. Perhaps you would decide this instantaneously or instead over a period of time (but no time). Know that when it is right for your individual progress, the decision is then made and the connection and the new growth both 'within' and out will never, ever fade.

This link lies deep inside. It is the inner desire to be found, to belong and not to hide from the love and light that is everywhere, in every place of existence and in every living thing. If you are 'ready' and wish to progress, perhaps you have already passed one of the creator's tests? Who knows what this could be? Is it something to overcome, or a sin to redress? Or maybe it is to serve in another way, to help your fellow beings? There could be too many reasons to mention, but on the soul level you would know the where and also the reason why you have been born to shine, to progress and to grow.

When your task is done, your Ascension and the tunnel of

light will direct you elsewhere so that you will 'all' be together in the universal one's care. The new home of love and light will be a vibration so 'sweet' and beautiful. There has been nothing else to compare to it.

So you see, the tunnel of light is made of love and it also proves you are living ... and also remain 'ALIVE'. Never be frightened or forgo your trust because within the darkness, just look for the 'speck' of light. It will shine brighter than ever ... more than anything you have ever seen or desired.

Those who have entered the tunnel (before their time) can give you a glimpse of what is in store for you and your soul, your consciousness, and your mind. These people were chosen to then return and give messages of love. They signal to others you do go on and on and if you have lived your life with love and light and have not denied yourselves or said, 'No hope'.

So, think with an open mind and not just from the head, and ask your heart if there is truth in these following words. "The oxygen deprivation before bodily death causes the rushing sensation and the tunnel is also caused by the shock of being brought back from the so-called dead."

Someone who has 'experienced' the tunnel of love and light knows in their heart what is the truth. It is down to all individuals to believe whether a soul actually returns from life's tree or if these are just words from this pen to confirm their own dark side of 'them'. Remember, we do not call or condemn those who have shut out or closed the door, but remind them all to realize, that to change or be different really is no chore.

David, it is your time to go now and chapter Eight to now debate. This Chapter is to be called, 'THE MIRACLE OF YOU'. In this, we will expand on new information so please keep strong; be strong ... for you are <u>strong</u>. Remember each of you has the immense power of love and light inside you, it is your very being and will see you through every difficulty that may surround you at this or at any point of your life.

Perhaps you are suffering so much pain (in some way), or whether it is ache or search for something that seems so very much in vain. Maybe it is a goal or desire to know the truth and find the 'real' you? Well, here is our promise ... you will finally succeed! Simply be true by living the reality of you. In love, light, peace, and truth, may God bless you all. Please go and...

EXPLORE

With a difference of opinion and in confusion different 'stories',
Leads the mind and heart astray, to the ugliness and the gory.
By changing and also thinking, 'Oh, that's a wonderful theory',
Will give you all the chance, to acknowledge the eternal glory.

Open up and understand ... and to offer outstretched hands,
To grow and know together, for love and light to then expand.
And brighter they will become, on this new level of vibration,
Linking every heart and land, the whole world and all its nations.

Then you'll really see, for your 'core' wants to explore,
Of the when and the way ... and also the what for.
So, discover your real 'self', and the inner one true goal,
Then you will find the truth ... that through your heart you save your soul.

Wonderful! Thank you and bless you too my friends and family. Please feel my love that I am sending to you, always and forever.

CHAPTER EIGHT: 'THE MIRACLE OF YOU'

Saturday 2nd November 1996

COMMUNICATION: *David, you do not need to say or do anything. We had heard when your heart and mind calls us from so near and far as the door of communication is always open and ajar.*

We have just seen the flowing colors from your heart as they 'beam' outward. A brilliant 'yellow' is shining and gleaming to push aside any barriers or inner shields (that now decay) for the light and truth is all around you, just as it is also inside us all.

Your meditation today has given you some answers you seek. These will come true because you deserve it to. We do not mean a material gain should always be sought but you will be given a helping hand. You will know when this is the case because it will surprise you, for it will come from another land! Never feel that what is being done is in vain because you have already touched so many souls over different terrains. What do we mean by this?

Do you remember in Pathway how we explained our task was to expand the truth and light to other places and galaxies, and to also help millions of beings unlike any of you? Well, we have also learned from your thoughts and experiences and have relayed much of this to others, so they also digest what is happening above and inside your planet.

It is from a layman's perspective that is just as important as any scientist or scholar, so be proud ... but there is no need for you to shout or 'holler'. The feelings and thoughts that have coincided from within and around you (and from other hearts too) have been digested and evaluated for your progress and for other species of light too. We are all 'one', no matter who or what we are, or in whatever task that is undertaken in life.

Deliverance of Love, Light and Truth

Okay, now Chapter Eight. This will bear no illusion or inner/outside confusion. We mentioned earlier that we will share new information within this chapter and this will aid you and help many others to continue to grow. First of all, we have a poem to quench your thirst for knowledge and also make people think about life's senses. It is called 'Momentum'.

MOMENTUM

You move both in waves ... and upon levels of vibration,
In individual journeys when it should be of all nations.
But a time will soon arrive, when decisions will be made,
And it's up to you and all ... prepare right now, not haste.

You are all of 'light' ... 'beings' of beauty and such splendor,
Though like molecular structure, you can change just like the weather.
Some move so very quickly, and are powerful as lightning,
While other's drift like sand or fall like stones off mountains.

Your 'inner' light and life, is yours for growth and learning,
And by reading these new 'works', you can go on from all the yearning.
You can forgive and then forget, or retain the black and hate inside,
But in clouding out the light, you're only continuing to hide.

Together be in peace, and move forward now in motion,
Links to family and your friends, on the planes of association.
For there is where you'll find, the inspiration from true existence,
To uplift and direct away, the hate and pain and ignorance.

There are many who do believe and also desire to achieve,
But some want material gain, and in false 'Gods' that they do heed.
The truth is deep within, and not religions that cast the doubt,
For they confuse and bring those wars, and tears inside and out.

We can describe to you ... the acceleration to take place,

The Miracle of You

To catch those drops of grief, that fall down upon your face.
You and you alone, can increase the pace and share the 'Faith',
But you need to believe it first, for it to happen and take place.

When your true desire, is to 'open' and achieve,
You can then learn your one true truth, to believe and not to need.
That we are all from 'one', but in splitting up to divide,
You can wedge and close the door, to your heart and soul and eyes.

So, understand that love, yes, your love's a special 'key',
To the door of light and truth ... and eternity.
When placed into the door, turn the handle do not knock,
For God's door is forever open ... when your heart and souls unlocked.

Time that can't be hidden, and mistakes of recognition,
As millennium have but passed and developed all of the religions.
But the creator gave free-will, and the choices to all heed,
A task to understand ... love and light are all you need.

Know a poem contains the lines, you'll understand or then you won't,
But never pass your task, and never give up hope.
Just strive to eternal goal, that's within you and above,
Opportunities to then develop, to fly high on wings of doves.

Each step that you all take, each nightfall and 'Daybreak',
Just feel and love your life, and not just for living sake.
For you can all achieve, with belief in that you can,
Open the door unto your soul, for you're more than just 'Human'.

Thank you for those words and poem of love. It was so wonderful and the love it contained touched me deep inside my heart. (As I write this, the candle flame rose 8–10 inches high with the immense 'energy' and connection.)

Deliverance of Love, Light and Truth

COMMUNICATION: *The words we share are just a small helping hand my son. They can be used and digested right now or someone who is not quite ready can put them to one side.*

We now ask, what is the 'MIRACLE' of you? Well, we have previously described in Pathway that much information has been documented in various guises of so-called miracles as well as mysteries and the paranormal. We also explained that miracles were 'Natural Laws' which some of you may have misunderstood.

These natural laws are God's laws and miracles are now spoken of as just words from the past and that is all. Yet you are all a miracle just as every living thing in the universe is a miracle. This is because you live; you breathe and you are alive with the light and are with light. Indeed you are made from love from the supreme 'being' and are minute fragments from its very core, a Father/Mother giving consciousness to souls of millions and of new 'life' to billions.

Events that have changed history (yours and ours) and all the evolution of life beyond comprehension are caused by tiny 'miracles' in themselves. Even thoughts and feelings channelled through the mind and to the hearts center form action and reaction, something so simple in its process through and through. Know that the earth's tiniest insect or creature, or its tallest tree, or even all the 'life' within the countless galaxies, all stems from the miracle of love and light and so it will always be. Everything was and is, born from the core of the everlasting source.

Some thoughts of confusion flash through your mind. Why then is there hate or misguided feelings? Why are there such crossed 'wires' in an individual's life core and soul's matrix ... and the darkness and confusion of death, pain, and the destruction? A dear child of light therein lays the message. 'A special gift of 'free-will' was given to you all, so long ago so that you could all learn and grow, and for yourselves not to be vain, hateful, deceitful, or egotistical.

Yes indeed, the involvement of so many has diverted the right to wrong, which has in turn misguided the weak away from the strong. Now 'time' has been allocated to those who are confused, to live and learn again and come towards the light and the truth. Then they can return to the everlasting power 'coil' and matrix of love and light itself. This feeling is inbuilt, for there is the need for you all to Ascend and come off the rebirth cycle, whilst you are also protected by Ascended Masters of light, including Archangel Michael!

There is much for you all to learn and know but inside is the connection and it is there where the answers lie to everything that can ever be known. (To understand everyone is part of the universal life force and of the 'beyond' forever too). Okay David, time for you to relax now my son and I know such feelings of love are strong. All is revealed at a steady pace that is right for 'now', so there is no need to worry or ever ask "How?" Please know you are all so wonderful and are all individuals, yet as we reiterate once more you are 'all one'. So in peace and love and light, go forward in truth and go on for we believe in you. 'Till next time, goodbye.

PS. We are going to share a picture with you soon which you will need to see, but please wait until the next time, for this most beautiful scene.

Thank you all and bless all those who have drawn close to me. My light and my life I share with thee.

N.B.: I feel I need to include this extra information of a dream and meditation. These are two 'supplements' which somewhat divide this chapter, but I feel it is important to relate and share them with you now.

DREAM AND MEDITATION SUPPLEMENTS

Dream Supplement—Sunday Night 3rd November 1996

I went to bed about 11.00 pm and awoke at 2.45 am from the first experience/dream of the night. It was a message from the Transleátions.

This surprised me, because it is the first dream containing their 'Two Sister's symbol' for communication in approximately four months. This is their usual call sign expressing me to contact and 'open' up as soon as possible for them. This is significant because they usually leave time scales between the channelled messages / inner-dictation every 10-14 days. However, as I have stated before, it is normally a feeling within me that seems to indicate the time is right for me. What was so important for me to receive them again so soon? Here is the dream.

'There is an audience and it is like I am part of it, yet not. My vision draws closer to find I am on the stage. Then, I am above the stage, just watching. (Many of my precognitive dreams are also 'viewed' this way).

There was a competition and a man and lady stood side by side, as if in a 'game show' answering questions. As I gazed upon them the man's face, his facial features started to change slightly. Then as a few seconds more passed by they became identical. I said to myself, they look like 'Two Sisters'. Suddenly the man's hair started to recede, and he began to change again. His hair just at the back of his head was pulled into a pony tail. He then looked like a 'Colonial' French or Englishman of the 1880s? I noticed he had something in his right hand.

At this point, my vision drew back and zoomed ten to fifteen feet away and all the surroundings had altered. The man was in an open space (open wilderness), as if in Africa (?) and he lifted a long barrel (?) to his mouth. Then, strangely I became this man. This tube or barrel (like a blow horn) bellowed out when I blew into it. It was as if I'd been sounding a signal into the air. I started to spin in a clockwise direction, sounding a note to the world. Yes, I am signaling both to communicate and to receive.

The dream ended with a private message for myself. I then awoke both surprised and pleased with the dream. Soon after, I drifted off to sleep again wondering what else may they wish to say. I hoped I would soon find out.

Meditation from Saturday 9th November 1996 (2.10 pm–2.40 pm)

I opened with prayers of love and protection and took my consciousness to my heart's center. What followed was so wonderful and as I write about my experience, my eyes are still swollen from tears filled with the love, the universal loves within and around us all.

I found myself beside a pool of water in a most serene and beautiful place. Suddenly before me, shone a beautiful light ... golden and sparkling. From the horizon across the water there formed a bridge of light and a pathway for me to move forward.

I cannot say I 'stepped' upon the bridge because I was 'light' too (as my true 'self'), yet the feeling of this action was there. I then immediately became aware of the presence of Angelic beings either side of me. They gently held my hand as if to carry me along the golden bridge and into the most radiant and brilliant light above it.

The peace and tranquillity engulfed me and the light seemed to surround us all as if we were in a mist. This then cleared to reveal the most amazing scene. In front and below and to the left and right as far as I could see, were row upon row of books. More volumes and works of literature than I could have ever imagined or seen before. I had this tremendous feeling this unique place contained something very special.

Somehow my consciousness and vision seemed to focus inward upon the meaning and the reason of this place. It was then that I realized its purpose. This was no ordinary library, for it was the Akashic Records! [49] (PICTURE FIFTEEN: 'THE AKASHIC RECORDS'.) To be present and convey my feelings of being 'there' are so hard to describe, and I hope what I have drawn can touch your heart.

I then seemed to be able to gaze further into the distance to a 'wall' of yellow light. My vision seemed to go inside it and I saw, 'PATHWAY'! (The first channelled book from the Trans-leátions). The book glowed and sparkled to acknowledge and make me understand it would be published and that it would take its small place amongst the knowledge and wisdom of Light.

Suddenly the book appeared in my hands and a strange thing occurred for I found myself standing inside the back of a huge 'lorry' (vehicle) which was decorated in the colors of the front cover of 'Pathway'. Inside of me I knew a 'being' of light was driving this vehicle, and we were traveling past many people who stood by the side of the road. They were those souls who wanted to

Deliverance of Love, Light and Truth

learn, who needed help and who had also come to understand.

As I stood at the tailgate of the lorry (which was laden with copies of Pathway) they began to fly out towards those in need, so that they could grow and know too. To my right-hand side stood a small boy with ripped clothes. He was both cold and hungry (spiritually not physically) and our eyes met as the lorry stopped. I jumped down and knelt beside him. I hugged him, and he asked me, "May I see?" I replied, "You will see, you will feel and you will be okay. All the nourishment and all your needs will be met in the light."

I gave him a copy of Pathway. "This will help you find the answers you need. Those things, which are already in your heart." (A feeling of love so immense came to both of us but it is so hard to describe such joy). I then went back to the tailgate, and yet I suddenly began to view this scene from space, above the earth. The lorry had encircled the world and was parked above it. Strangely it was as if I was also watching myself too.

I climbed on top of the lorry and opened a copy of Pathway. It revealed a soft pink rose, which emerged, from the centre pages and I held it up high. The rose petals opened further to shed millions and millions of roses and petals that filled the 'space' around and over the earth like a blanket of love and protection. This rose I held received a 'beam' of light (much whiter than white) from above me and into its center. This light appeared to drop a clear substance onto one of its petals. I paused to look at it and I wondered, was it water, a drop of rain?

It became heavier and heavier on the edge of the petal as if gravity began to pull it down into an oval or pear shape figure. It glowed like a beautiful clear quartz crystal shining in the moonlight. I became aware it was not a drop of rain or even a crystal, but that it was a tear of God's love. I gasped inside as it then fell down towards the earth. At this precise moment all the roses and their petals began to release millions of tears of love into (and onto) the earth-plane. Tears of hope, strength and wisdom are here for us all. (It is so difficult to explain in words how this felt).

Another 'beam' of light emerged from a magnificent rainbow and it enveloped and protected me. Each color was so individually vibrant, yet they were all different levels of resonance and energy, to then become one with me. My vision, (as if now outside myself again) watched closely as my 'aura' became filled with such strength and encouragement and beautiful love. At this point I could see and feel my own hearts center spiraling like a 'coil' with a separate rainbow within 'me'.

After this I became aware that I needed to return to the physical and I did this on the multi-colored cord of light. However, before I did so, I could see a heavenly 'Star' on my right piercing the realms of my consciousness. It shone so brightly but then faded, and I felt a message had come to me to say the whole world is going to 'experience' something. It would change people's minds and views and was going to 'open' many hearts too!

PICTURE FIFTEEN: 'THE AKASHIC RECORDS'

I do not know what it is but have a very strong feeling that it is within a tragedy and a release of love in world mourning.

However, it is within our time frame and is not too far away. Oh, dear Lord, I feel that someone very special will be crossing over into your loving care. How soon will this be dear Lord, one year or two? (I then returned to my physical embodiment).

This experience, as many before, will stay with me forever and I am so glad to be able to share it with you all. Remember, the love and answers to 'everything' lie within you. Just look into your heart and you will see. As my family and friends from other dimensions say, love and light, peace and truth are free, for all to see and all to be!

AFTER THE MEDITATION

Having paused and reflected on the meditation, I now realized that the experience of the beautiful scene was from the connection with the Trans-leátions. It was as if what I had experienced was prepared (prior) for me as many things are for us all!

I then asked, "Please see that my hand is now ready for the pen to flow. My heart is open too for you, and I know I am protected with your love and from my guides and teachers who have gathered close to me at this time. Bless you all ... your son David.

COMMUNICATION: *We are here my son and our cords of light will always connect us.*

Your love that shines and glows has touched us deep within and when your tears fall as you surveyed the 'scene', you had shone brilliant gold and fluorescent green. Colors in beautiful radiance were wrapped around your core, where the love of God is magnified even more and more.

When your hands were held and you soared so high, it was us that stood by your side! David, please dry your eyes. You do not need to cry, and you're aware that we know and also understand why. Within yourself, you knew you were safe ... and where you traveled will never be in darkness or hate or sin because we are all 'one' from the creator's center within. That's better, a little smile. We know you become upset because of the 'love' that is so beautiful and serene it can never be quantified, depleted or be mean. Can we share the reason why you now laugh?

Deliverance of Love, Light and Truth

You have drawn a picture overlooking the divine mist ... were the wings you observed just an illusion or some may say delusion? No! You know that we are beings of light and do not need wings to take flight but what we wanted to show you the 'light' comes in countless forms with many meanings will be given to all.

We could be seen to be 'Angels' or 'Ascended' Masters or whatever names someone decides to place upon us. All we ask is for you all to live and learn and trust. Know that the way someone learns and 'opens up' or 'sees' differently to another does not matter, for one cannot ever condemn someone for his differences if they live in truth and peace. We are light and you have seen part of our 'original' form that has developed over the millennium. You now also know we are close by those who require our help and guidance even though they do not know our name, or where we are from or of what our true task is (yet).

This of course will be understood, and they will know this when they have opened their heart and digested the truth to follow their own Pathway. Sometimes darkness can overcome and confuse those who try to grow in the love and this is why (as we have briefly explained before) the first collated works through you is not on the bookshelves this very day.

However, the doubts and greed in its many 'guises' forget that God's love and light are supreme and when individuals are growing (because they want to) and when they are surrounded by love and light connected to an open heart they can never be pushed aside. You will see.

As you write David, it could be deemed by some that this chapter or phase of the book is disjointed or unconnected. The reason we say this is those who depict this may feel this way about it until the realization of what they are and of what the 'Miracle of You' means on many levels have been understood.

We talk about the physical in so many contexts and manifestations, but today (along with your meditation) it can show many others that their consciousness, their mind, their souls are all part of this energy and beauty.

Humankind understands little of what the 'mind' can do. Of course, people will often wish to forget the mind, but it is so

The Miracle of You

beautiful. Appreciate it is so much more than what you think or say or do. Through your spiritual development you can experience more of what can really be achieved beyond the physical plane (which can act like a magnet or an imaginary trap), but this provides an opportunity to experience a point of transfer of your consciousness to the inner 'beyond'. The mind is the connection and learning centre or base, a point in which you can expand in more ways than can be imagined.

This is truly the 'Miracle of You', but we can also never deny the beauty of 'creation' which surrounds your light, the 'body' ... a shell that enables you to live, to breathe, to kiss, to cry, to laugh and also to 'physically' die. Why? Well, many know of the death and rebirth 'cycle'. However, the earlier chapters of this book may alter the way they comprehend and understand what can be transformed, their very nature and infinite divine essence. Not to return to the physical form ever again, but to remain and see forever inside the light ... not to languish or be forlorn.

So, the goal has been set and the vibrations of planet earth and your people are changing. How you proceed with the here and now and in the 'future' will go a long way to depict (in a sense) the earth-plane's advancement and duration. No doubt, many souls will go on and on and will 'Ascend' to the new dimension, and they will rejoice forever together with the universal beings of countless worlds and nations.

Well, David, today is almost drawn to a close and you have experienced much both 'within' and around from your head down to your toes. Also, with the gathering of many (that you have not seen) and who were close by you, they too have been showered by the love you have described from up above so serene.

Finally, there are two things we need to close on. Know that the dream you hadn't expected was no more than a reminder we are with you even though you 'sleep'. Your physical body may be tired, but your soul flies each night to learn and to touch our love that is always yours to keep.

Know too, the 'instrument' of communication bellowing out loud and around and around forever in true circles will reach out so far and wide. The sound of love will flow across your world just like it's many seas and tides. Also, the first dream you received last

Deliverance of Love, Light and Truth

night was a gift for you to express the knowledge and wisdom you have, so that people will know the truth. Maybe one day the 'platform' is where you will go?

An opportunity will present itself soon and you can reveal so much from your heart and it will quench many people's 'thirst' for wisdom and strength. This will help them each day and help them on their way. You will see ... so always trust and believe in the love, light, peace and truth and in 'me'. Forever, your friend,

'Millanderer'. Goodbye until next time my son, then chapter Nine will then begin.

You will always be in my heart. Thank you so very much.

CHAPTER NINE: ENDEAVOR

Sunday 24th November 1996

I am sorry it has been a while since we last spoke. May I hear you now, so that Chapter Nine can begin. I wait for you, yet somehow know you are already here.

COMMUNICATION: *My dear son. It is so good to draw as close as we can ... to enable you to expand and feel what lies within you. We also wish for you to understand even more than you did before or ever thought you could.*

As your heart lifts and soars beyond the normal feelings of life and the troubles of your earthly strife, try to forgive and forget past ills, be still and 'pause'. Embark on this journey of (and for) knowledge and wisdom so many others can grow too. Your heart and mind are shining so brightly they now both smile as one ... with such laughter and love to fill our souls. After all, your progress and for the many too is our goal! We desire to teach, help, share and guide all those who wish to enter the light forever.

Every one of you resemble billions of shining, twinkling stars that pulsate and shine light ... each is a passing or ongoing flicker of the creator's heart that is eternal, forever giving out love, peace, and truth. You are all so beautiful, just as all life is. Just recognize yourself ... your real 'self' and your soul within and you can then move forward from any hate or decaying sin. Choices will always remain yours to take; after all isn't your life and soul and your own eternity at stake? Why do we say these things today? Why not indeed ... other than to explain and cast out the myths of misapprehension, the deceit, or any greed.

Deliverance of Love, Light and Truth

Today we have started Chapter Nine. Will it lead a single soul or guide the many to the 'heaven' and the 'divine'? We shall then see who takes the advice on board and also those who throw it away or place it with other guidance just to hoard. Perhaps there is confusion, 'Shall I follow that?' or 'What direction shall I take?' Do those who 'open' now cry or shout in dismay, "Where do I look and what shall I find?" Mm, David, those very same words of a poem you had written a short while ago are again revealed at such an appropriate time.

Okay, this Chapter will be called ENDEAVOR. It will contain what someone could wish or ask for, or it may make some of you quite sad. There are three parts to this chapter and part one (today) is to explain some more of the soul's continuing pathway. A path that each of you has been sent to embark upon, but to undertake it will always emerge from your own accord.

Part two is to follow another day. This will explain and help others to put some more of their misapprehensions away. A question and answers session will be so right here, so prepare some notes on what you wish to know for a clearer understanding of the black and white.

Part three will subsequently conclude this second book. This will then lead you onto book three of this spiraling information and loving network. We will give you as much time as you require before that begins ... it could be one year, 10 years or 3 scores or more, but when <u>you</u> are ready the seal will be broken for 'new' rays of love and light to flood in.

Higher and higher the vibrations and frequency will be known if you only endeavour to expand. Try not to retreat into your shell but instead unconditionally give out your love and light so you could be taking flight. Now let us lead on with part one.

You were all 'born' of light, fragments of energy like rays of love which have been emitted, radiating, and spiraling from the Almighty, the creator. Oh, what a most beautiful sight. Such splendor! But, what have you done over many millennia? People have lived to hate and fight as well as to give and share and partake the immense energy of love ... which is your destiny and goal and very 'birth right'.

Endeavor

That said, what quest and search has the individual soul begun over your many lifetimes? How many attempts does it take to become? Do not misunderstand by what we have said here, for your physical 'body' dies and it decays but your true self is never, ever 'dead' as we have stated many times before. Furthermore, your gift of free will is often mistaken for lust when all that you need to move on to the life everlasting is for you to trust.

So, you have to begin somewhere and that journey is within your 'Self'. You can then progress and go on to endure those exterior influences which try to dissuade you away from this. It's these that cause the pain, confusion, and mistrust too. We, of course, know this is not new information for some of you. We reiterate such words because many of you can stop someone else from feeling down and so blue. Just return to the core for your own everlasting truth of you and find that you will no longer feel confused or wander aimlessly lost.

What is certain is that as each of you crossover, and are 'ready' to stay and make the choice not to return to the earth-plane, then your desire is granted. Do not be unsure with what we say. You are never told you must return for that is not the way. You have this inbuilt understanding and know what you have to do, both for your own growth and maturity as a soul. Perhaps it is in further 'service' whereby helping others you ultimately help 'yourself'.

So, the continuous path is never set in stone, but the wish is yours 'within' to move on to your new 'home'. Will this help with those who embark upon their inner-path or, will this rattle the cage of reality, shaking it up to cause the mind to swell?

We shall now move on to describe and explain more about the second wave of Ascension. As it approaches its correct place(s), its vibrations will be mirroring the spectrum of light sent out from God's love. It will call both the individual and the many in one brief fragment and pulse of a pure energized beam, for the entrance and crossing 'over' to the eternal Heaven, is no dream.

Be prepared. Yes, prepare with your hearts open wide for over that night so many will take flight. They will have moved forward so well they can help prepare for the 3rd and 4th Ascension wave. This will be more clearly defined nearer the chosen 'place' and 'time' of course both through and also by, the divine.

Deliverance of Love, Light and Truth

What you all do now needs to be undertaken with truth and dignity. Please know these are not commands but describe ways forward for those who have been confused or dazed or lost over many millenniums. Therefore, friends, guides, teachers of every shape, color, nation or creed, are guided by your feelings of love within. Then you will know what you can share to help others or even your next of kin. Perhaps you could even help an insect or animal in peril, or even support Mother Nature by shining more brightly like a beautiful flower. Expand your vibration within then stretch and cast out what seems so restrictive and tight like an unknown second skin. The denser, heavier 'you' can then be cast-off as a false shadow.

Indeed, you can all become the beacons that emit light beyond your home and country, if you only stopped to push aside the fear that makes you run and hide. David, a dear friend of yours said something that touched your heart recently. (It falls into this second book, but it is not quite ready to be shared with the many in its entirety). We have discussed this with his guides and can partly reveal the thoughts that expand deep inside your mind, perhaps to ponder and be weighed up by many of humankind. 'Do you enjoy what might happen ... as much as you fear what might happen?' This question can relate to a many areas in your lives. Your job, your quest, your goal, your journey or perhaps it is your desire to comprehend the reality of your relationship to embrace the creator within all life. The above question may mean one thing to one person and something completely different to another. Each of you are individuals as we have mentioned before but you are also part of the 'one', as we all hope to always be.

Okay David, next time we communicate we'll move on to your question and answers session which you will need to prepare. This is to dispel any fears, not to frighten or to scare. These new questions will come from your heart and the answers and information are for the many who will want to read and hear. So, until the pen flows again, always strive to be 'lighter'. In peace and love and in truth please do share, always together and forever we will care.

Thank you from my heart, forever!

Saturday 30th November 1996 (1.45 pm)

I feel I have to share some thoughts with you before we begin the second part of chapter nine. I guess what I hope to be revealed will be new information, yet am not naive enough to expect too much.

As we have heard before, 'you cannot learn any more than the level you have reached'. This profound statement which is also included in Book 1 came from the early teachings I received from 'Sue', a wonderfully gifted clairvoyant/ medium. She has such an open-heart and mind and truly is a guide on this earth-plane for the many whom she comes into contact with.

What I would like to convey is that we are all at different learning stages or levels of vibration/energy. Someone cannot be deemed better than another because our own development is for progress sake. If we are true to ourselves then we can admit this or acknowledge it in a sense, and then hopefully we can all move forward.

So, whether this information is with further knowledge and wisdom and experiences (or if it is just a repetition of what we think or know in our hearts) does not matter. This is because the human race is unique, yet we are also born no less a being of 'light,' a child of the creator, God, the Great White Spirit.

So, in this sense we should be able to help each other in what we feel, say, and do. Not chastise, condemn, or hate someone else for his or her appearance, beliefs or for their feelings on what true existence really is.

Well, the Trans-leátions have requested I prepare some questions, so they can relay their 'findings' and truth to help the many. These are from my heart. Some of you may already feel you know the answers, or perhaps they will give you another avenue or explanation to consider. Hopefully, you will at least find them interesting! Maybe you will think you don't believe any of it, or state you feel that it's different to what you have already learned. Who knows?

What I do believe is the answers lay inside us all, deep within our soul's and heart's center. Perhaps you can journey 'within' to expand your thoughts and feelings further, to help you fulfill your own desire and quench your own thirst for wisdom and truth. It could truly put you in touch with that tranquility and peace that does exist and forever will be part of you ... and me and of every living thing.

Okay it is soon time to 'link' and for the pen to flow. Firstly though, a short meditation for you.

Meditation 2.00 pm to 2.20 pm

I am in the sea, which is beautiful and clear. Then, I merge with this pure ocean, breathing as one, gliding along with the waves in motion.

There is 'life' all around me, many living things, and creatures. I drift upon a turtle, and I cling to its shell as we go deeper towards the seabed. I observe beautiful mermaids. Suddenly, I sense soft music and it rings inside of me bringing an overwhelming feeling of peace. There is a light shining brightly and within it I see some stairs that lead upward. There are pillars, one on each of the step. Above these are crystals, emitting light of another frequency and vibration. Such warmth and love emanate from them.

I knew this was a special place, for as I moved upon the steps, another light ... like a star, floated towards me, and we seemed to blend as one energy. After this, I saw a decayed apple beneath me. I touched it, and it returned to a new and full freshness ... returning to the tree, a tree of light and life!

The apple is then expelled upward from the centre of the tree just like the 'star' light I first saw. It floats away, but I need to follow. Suddenly I am on the back of a dolphin, weaving along and up through to the surface of the sea so that I become this resonance too. As I am light, I am able to surge high into space and beyond dimensions to the universal connection ... drifting, merging as 'one'. Within me I hear the words, 'Welcome my Son'.

I sense a magnificent presence. Such tranquility and stillness descend upon me ... and my vision becomes clearer as Dear Lord Jesus stands before me. I kneel and kiss His feet, and gasp, 'Oh Father'. Love surrounds my whole being, and my tears fall over His feet. *"Stand up my Son. You are part of me as I am part of you, so do not weep."*

'But I have sinned Father, why do I sin so?' *"Because you have 'tried' to 'live'. Nothing is wrong, just continue to grow. Come with me..."* As He held my hand, immense energy flowed into every

Endeavor

fiber of my being, touching the core and existence of my heart and my life and my soul.

We enter a 'garden' of Eden, yet even though there are no trees and flowers, I have an indescribable feeling of ‚peace and of love. I stayed here for a short time. Then, in the distance, I saw an archway and am beckoned over to it. Inside me I hear, *"Please return to your temporary home, for where you have just been lays here for you all eternally."*

I feel I do not wish to go, but in front of me, I sense a desk and a candle and am handed a white feather. *"Please continue to write from your heart so that others may be helped to open theirs. Continue now and go back to your task, for your pen to flow for all know."* I drift further and further away ... becoming dense and heavy, a slower vibration in returning to myself. Wow!

How do I feel now? Sad ... yes, I am really sad to be away from this beautiful love I have just experienced; and yet …. I am so happy to know this is within me ... and within you and every living thing around us all! Okay, time to move on and the questions to begin, so now lift up your hearts so that they may sing.

Please, dear Trans-leátions hear my heart and cry to link with you. I wish to understand 'more', and I weep by asking the when and how and why? My friends and family, you are so special to me for you are all part of the eternal living tree. Please come to thee for I hope these questions can reveal the solutions to many of our needs.

COMMUNICATION: *We are here dear child, and we hear the call of your open heart. Allow us to share our hope and wishes, for all to become 'one' and never part.*

As you have just experienced, the future awaits each form of life and it's so tranquil. Unconditional love is an elixir of nourishment, the eternal source that is our creator of truth and of light. Open your heart further now David, and reveal your thoughts and questions.

We shall endeavor to help you with our guidance and lead you all away from any pain. Do you require an instant relief, or a release over time? Obviously, each of you are vastly different in character and personality yet you are also all of 'one' too. We will now respond, so let the questions flow naturally from deep within.

Question 1: "Many people ask about their guides, teachers and helpers from the many planes and levels of vibration, but why does this happen? Do our guides choose us or do we choose them? Please can you explain more of this to us?"

Answer: *Much more can be said than in the few questions here, but we shall try to explain 'simply' for those who are just beginning to grow.*

We are all 'one' ... connected to each other, and so as an individual becomes stronger you can grow further and higher upon your evolution as a light 'being' and as a soul. As your vibration level increases further, so does your need for growth. This brings the need for assistance both 'within' and 'out'. This help is never refused, but you learn what you need to at each part of your life (and lives), whatever is needed for your spiritual development.

Guides, teachers, and family are of course unquantifiable, and they come in countless ways, shapes and forms and for many reasons. Each has their own special quality and it can be said, their own purpose. You, yourself know this David and that is why we are here and you are holding the pen at this precise moment.

It must be said that none of you (or any 'light 'being') is forced to help and nurture a 'soul' (or any other life force) because free will is universal from the creator's heart ... and always has been and always will be. It is the misuse of one's energy that cannot and will not be sustained.

The presence of light helps in many ways but often go unnoticed. This is because an individual's sensitivity has been hidden or disguised by what you place around you through the way you think or feel, or by the karmic 'layer' that surrounds your heart. Everyone has his or her own 'guidance', but it is required to be called upon in truth and in love and in peace.

There is much confusion over where such guidance comes from, and it is true that you have to be careful when you open up to let the love flow 'in' ... or when you share it too. Negative energy is always attracted to the positive and for this reason, you must protect yourself with prayer, decrees and the light and love of your mind and heart. However, we need to expand on this. Others say that if you lower yourself in vibration or desire you drift or enter the lower worlds/dimensions. Of course, this does happen, only the soul will decree that it is definitely wrong or an inevitable learning process?

Make no mistake, everyone needs to aim for the highest level they can reach, which is the divine ... the infinite. Try to live and help in all the ways that you can, included venturing towards the lower realms too, both to give guidance and assistance where needed most. Also when your light has been offered to defend truth and light alongside Archangel Michael and his legions of guardian angels.

So, it becomes clear that only in truth should you enter lower realms for those correct reasons. If your desire was to remain there, then that would be different. Everyone, during day or night, has his or her job to do in the form of light. What we would also say is that you all work with your guides and teachers, and it is not all one-way traffic by design or manufacture ... it is both giving and receiving. Guides, teachers and your family and friends obtain just as much nourishment and love from you too, as they know the individual is growing, and they feel your love that gets brighter. It helps them and also sustains them too. All are 'one' and one is part of all.

Know that the negativity and darkness is as much part of 'everything' as is the positive energy and the light. Does this sound strange or conflicting advice? Please consider the following ... aren't your atoms made of positive and negative protons? Likewise, isn't a phrase 'opposites attract' very much in evidence within your world when two souls slowly fall in love? (Or out of love as the case may be!)

Everything is for growth and for you to grow side by side each other or instead ... if you need to be alone. You all have your own direction and road to embark upon which will always lead to the right pathway, if you have and are open to 'love'.

Finally, we need to say the greatest teacher is your own inner flame of love and light, because it is your heart's connection to the creator itself. In reality everything else should become secondary and for additional guidance only.

Question 2: Many people seem confused regarding 'other' guidance and over what path to follow in their quest for soul growth or in service to others. Some are even unsure what 'faith' to follow, especially with new philosophy coming to the 'fore' in the Age of Aquarius. What should someone do … what should they pursue?"

Answer: *'Intuition'. Your sixth sense is often hidden, denied, or pushed to one side. That 'gut' feeling can tell you whether something is right for you. However, there isn't wrong or right in development of one's <u>exterior</u> knowledge. Whatever is right for that individual, then circumstances in their life (and what they are pursuing) will materialise for them to flourish.*

You are right in regard to those outside influences and of course it is part of your nature 'within' to try out many things in your life. We do not just mean in the spiritual or religious sense either. How would you know what something is like or whether it is right for you if you have not tried it? Nevertheless, it is important to listen to 'the whisper of truth inside yourself because make no mistake, if something is wrong then the outcome of such a road will manifest itself in its many guises to steer you and the negative forces away from what is right for you. (But only if you allow it.)

Basically you need to identify your feelings and purpose within your life. Follow your intuition but at the same time consider your actions and thoughts and deeds and how they will affect others. You cannot proceed blindly with thoughts only for yourself and your own 'gain'.

Simply trust in yourself and God, and remember, if the actions or path you are pursuing remains one of love, truth and light, it helps others and also feels right for you, then follow it, for it will be true!

Question 3: "When a friend, relative or loved one (be it human or an animal or any living thing) is ill, in pain or suffering, what is the reason? Have they done something wrong? Why do they have to go through what they do? Why do we have to live in pain that way? If an illness should lead to their loss, and they have gone, why is it sometimes so, so difficult for life to go on?"

Answer: *David, much of what you ask to be explained here has been covered in Pathway and earlier in this book. However, please remember (and you know this) do not fear 'death'. It is rebirth and part of your soul's cycle. However, it is now the continued rebirth that needs to be addressed and overcome through the souls' progress.*

Illness, pain and suffering are caused in many ways and are transferred onto one or more (or all) of your bodies (mental, physical, emotional or etheric/astral). When this occurs within all four, there is a deep-rooted problem that really needs working upon and for it to be cleansed. (In the sense of bringing light and also making oneself a lighter vibration.)

Your ills, your pain or your suffering can be in any of your bodies but generally, if one particular one is in a state of ill health (of miss-aligned vibration) then it will also manifest itself in some way or another within one of the others. For instance, if you mistreat your body then the physical will only ever appear in that manifestation of how you have treated it. As all bodies are corrected, you're emotional, mental and astral bodies can become imbalanced too, thus creating a vicious circle.

Many forget the physical is a beautiful temple that gives and receives love. It enables you to eat and breathe whilst on the earth-plane and yet you cram toxins deep into your veins and your very core which in turn reveals itself in the way we have described. Through smoking, taking drugs and the way and 'what' you eat and drink ... maybe (just maybe) this will make just one of you think.

We are not saying you should all become nuns or monks in the way you live, as the individual always retains a choice of course. This line of thought could be said to be very basic but maybe it needs to be stated like this again ... if only for the guidance of the few who do not know this, or who try to block it out of their minds.

When darkness enters your being in the form of depression, stress, or via anger, hate, loss, or feelings of unhappiness in any form *then the answer is to simply remember <u>love</u>. Yes, remember to love life ... for 'life' itself, because this can never be erased from the heart. Therefore, please find the strength within you all at times of struggle, pain, or confusion.*

Simply believe and know you can never be 'alone', even when you think you are. This is also the case when nobody else seems to care or understand you or is beyond 'hearing' (what you call) your normal lines of communication or touch. Know that distance or time is irrelevant. Harsh to say, but this is true. Nothing can break the hand of true friendship and true love and care connected to and from someone ... or for something that has touched your heart.

Question 4: Why did God, the Creator ... the Great White Spirit create 'life'?

Answer: *David, what made you ask this? How strange? Throughout the universe, billions of worlds and countless 'beings' believe they are part of some sort of experiment. (What thoughts does this conjure up?) If we say to you that the creator is pure 'love' and light and energy, what would this also mean?*

Likewise, when something physically dies, does it not give 'food' or life or to change the energy and vibration of other things around it? The 'energy' (of the body) goes on to exist in other ways so it gives nourishment to the earth, to other living things and whatever comes into contact with it. Its soul energy is elsewhere. Can you comprehend this?

Life is eternal. Life has always been in existence and shall be in one form or another. Do not put constraints on your mind and the thoughts that enter it. The creator is 'life' and hence by emitting energy gives and sustains life. Remember, life can have no timescale, and is without an ending or final destruction.

Since the source of all things is love ... the love that is given 'out' has also always been so. In the same way you could also ask how and when were solar systems and galaxies that exist beyond your own come into being. Let us simplify this further.

When a mother gives birth to her child it is a continuance, an expansion of love ... a 'life' created by love. Therefore, love creates eternal life.

David, it's time to pause for a while to reflect on what has been said and to prepare for what comes next, with more questions to ask and answers to be given. In addition, decide whether to include your 'Butterfly' image as you may like to share with others, and this will help show them what we mean.

We want to say that we are always watching over you, just as all guides, teachers, friends, and family watch over every individual. In love, light, peace, and truth. Bless you all, from Millanderer.

Thank you and bless you too.

Wednesday 27th November 1996

Dream Supplement: 'The Butterfly'

On the night of 27th November, I awoke from a deep sleep during which I had witnessed a clear outlined image of a butterfly on some sort of canvas? (PICTURE SIXTEEN: 'BUTTERFLY'). I lied still in bed, and it felt like a precognitive 'scene', just as I would normally 'view' a future event. My initial thoughts were that it could be symbolic, as if a transformation is to take place, and it didn't' take long before I would find out!

The next day I realized I had experienced a precognition for myself from Spirit. More proof I was being watched over, just as we all are. Let me explain myself. I had recently left employment as a carer in a residential home (for adults with learning difficulties) and had just gone back into the Financial Services Industry as a Financial Consultant.

In this role, I received over 250 new clients whom I had never met. On the 28th of November 1996 I traveled to a client's house to discuss their business. Mrs K invited me into their living room and there, to the side of the room was a large 2ft plastic and cloth butterfly, attached to the side of a 'standard' lamp! As soon as I saw this, I knew its message! The flashing dream image was re-enforcing my faith and belief. Yes ... the love and light are always with us whenever and wherever we go! (Thank you Spirit).

On the 5th of December 1996, I went back to their home and they gave me permission to take a photograph to substantiate the 'proof'.

PICTURE SIXTEEN: 'BUTTERFLY'

Saturday 9th December 1996 1.15pm

Again, I feel the need to include something else into this book. An experience of my own mind and heart to share with you. I hope you can enjoy and understand it.

Short Meditation:

I am encased in light ... because I am light. Some other forms of illumination descend from above and they begin to swirl and encircle me. It is as if I can 'see' inside them. Within this moment I am overwhelmed with peace and love. Then, everything clears to reveal, wait for it ... fairies! They are so beautiful, and I know they have come to help me.

Suddenly I drift upward as if becoming one with them. It is as if I resonate at a similar frequency and brightness and also their size too. We move in unison forming a cross of light, and then forward and upward towards a brilliant light containing great power. As we enter this I find myself coming to a halt.

I sense a circle of energy drawing closer and it begins to spin. Within this are my family and friends. Stillness overcomes me for as <u>they</u> spin around, light emanates and flows toward and into me. I am now in the centre of the circle. I feel immense and incredible warmth but my words cannot begin to explain this feeling.

For some reason, I look up. Above me there is a large cross ... a crucifix. Jesus is upon the cross and I kneel before Him. "Dear Lord, I feel your love so much". Jesus suddenly stood before me, a light 'presence' I cannot describe. I start to cry, and a tear falls down my cheek. He holds out His right hand, catches my tear and it starts to change into a sparkling light, a light of love. He gives it back to me, placing it in my right hand. I ask him if I can give it to the world.

My tear, this loving light Jesus has returned to me, falls down to the earth. It encompasses and covers the ground like an 'aura' of light. Jesus then said, *"Now turn around my Son, and open your heart to see"*. I turned to find we were on higher ground. Below us, and as far as I could see ...were people. Millions upon millions of souls were coming to the light, like candle flames burning and flickering brightly. (PICTURE SEVENTEEN: 'SEA OF SOULS').

Jesus spoke again, *"Like billions of Stars, love and light is for all, and all will come my Son"*. He took my hand, and we drifted through and over some of these souls to a higher place. I sat down as he handed me a white feather and some parchment paper to keep. *"Continue your writing for the world, so they may see and read about the same love that resides in me, resides within you all. Please look..."* I looked upward as clouds and mist came over a horizon and a sudden crack of powerful 'thunder' ripped apart the Heavens. A shower of beautiful light immediately followed to burst through like a 'rainfall of tears' and these fell magnificently onto the earth below. I gasped at this a sudden explosion of brilliance. I briefly shielded my 'vision' from its intensity.(PICTURE EIGHTEEN: 'GOLDEN RAIN OF LOVE').

I gazed upon the earth. The world had become encompassed in a network of beautiful light, called the Ascension 'network'. The light then drifted up and along the Ascension cords. Oh, such wonder, beyond comprehension. Jesus spoke yet again, both into my heart and mind, *"All will come with open hearts and minds ... when the time is right."* (PICTURE NINETEEN: 'THE ASCENSION CONNECTION').

PICTURE SEVENTEEN: 'SEA OF SOULS'

There was a pause, before I started to float away with a feeling of deep love and immense compassion for us all. I knew that I had to return to my body but I desperately wanted to stay. It was not my 'time' of course, though one day, yes one day I hope and pray. So, I am light, and we are light, but I returned to my denser self. Dear Jesus, thank you so much from deep within my heart. To our friends and guides, family, and teacher's too ... may God' love be forever with you all.

It is now 2pm

Dear Trans-leátions , I hope and pray to connect our hearts and minds in love, light, and truth. Please help to ease someone else's pain of their body, heart or soul and guide them towards the answers that lay in their heart. Perhaps to even help them expand their search own 'within'. Please hear me this day.

Deliverance of Love, Light and Truth

PICTURE EIGHTEEN: 'GOLDEN RAIN OF LOVE'

PICTURE NINETEEN: 'THE ASCENSION CONNECTION'

COMMUNICATION: *We are here for you David, as you are part of us all and part of the 'one'. Know that every soul and living being has always has been and always shall be in reaching for their goal.*

We have been watching over you during your meditation/experience that you have just been through. It is so beautiful to see and feel the love Jesus has for us all. The creator's love flows through Him and all the Ascended Masters and it will continue to do so. Love and light are so immense (as you described), and is free for all who open to love and light. Jesus was, and still is, a wonderful, wonderful teacher and part of you all indeed. 'He' will always be ... for He is the SON.

Remember, by turning within yourself and touching your heart and soul's 'Flame', you are connecting with your higher-Self, your Christ Consciousness, and your living energy. So, the creator, the Great White Spirit, God (or whatever name you call him/her) is there ... within you, no matter what the color of your skin, creed or 'religion' you are or would prefer to be. If you believe, you will find Him for he is there inside you. Also, please know every living thing is connected together this way, as this is how it will always be. It is this truth you 'open' to, and the love you touch so deep both within and around you. This is the eternal source of all things.

David, recently you had been given a question (to be asked), but you did not know it at the time. Please ask it now.

Question 5: There are many single or married people who 'love' or are in love with more than one person, be it with someone else's husband or wife or 'partner'. I have been asked, "What is wrong or right?" Do they stay or do they take flight? (For so much 'pain' seems to be involved).

Answer: *David, what you ask is complex and yet, is also remarkably simple too. Is there a right or wrong answer here? By that statement, some will say we are sitting on the 'fence' in our reply but is that not the case, for the individual(s) concerned when they ask why?*

Love, as we have described in 'Pathway' and throughout all 'time', is a universal life force. It is a feeling and emotion and there is no right or wrong time when love becomes hardened and 'encased' or blossoms both around (or in) someone's heart and mind. Love can be buried deep and remain hidden until the correct moment when it surfaces with an eruption of joy or pain.

Some people state—and we have heard this many times before— that they cannot hurt another by a separation. Yet it can also be said that those who (through taking no action), are only trying to remain content and live with repressed feelings for another. So, who or what is right or wrong? Is there even a correct answer here? Well ... free will and choice is God's gift.

Endeavor

We have also said everyone should complete this 'life' cycle and do anything they wish to achieve, but without hurting anyone else if you can please. So, what is the individual prepared to give for a fulfilled heart? Does this give rise to someone else's pain, or does it mean that you should wave goodbye, on the wing of a prayer or plane?

Some may now think of this as a loss of the feeling deep inside their heart, which produces an ache and makes them feels sick 'inside' with worry or guilt. Is it plainly disguised? Remember, your lives are just a flicker of reality and 'real' time by minutes or hours does not exist as we have said before.

Love is never erased or forgotten. For when your family member or friend or beloved animal or pet 'crosses over', you will see them again that is for certain! Likewise, if someone were to connect and meet their 'soul mate' is it destiny? Whether you are to meet love within the physical dimension or when you cross over into the Ascended planes does not matter, because the connection is always there, deep within you on a 'soul' level. (Some may read this and understand straight away, for others perhaps another day).

Appreciate you are so diverse in character and makeup that what is important to one will not be to another. This is why the choice and decisions of life are down to you and you alone. No pressure is ever placed upon you but from yourself. You must always make your own decisions.

In terms of 'guidance', you can do this by listening to your heart. Is it, as we have said, part of your destiny or of those around you? Is it part of your karma or of those around you to feel lost, cold, or lonely? This may seem to be a strange statement because in love, light and truth you can never be those things. This is why we shall now ask you, are 'vows' meant to be broken or are they sacred to be observed? If not, what is their point?

David, you have asked a simple question (Q 5), yet it can lead to an answer that can be remarkably diverse. Our response is proposed by a poem to both the individual and the masses.

ANGUISH

Do you listen to your heart, or the mind for what you do?
Do you cry and simply wish, that you can just be 'you'?
And of this anguish and the pain, for the love I thought I'd found,
When faced with such decisions, will I be swallowed in the ground?

Well ... fate and destiny can be played, by the one and by you all,
But do you follow now or pause ... when you really hear love's call?
And is it right or wrong, to feel the way you do,
When God's word simply says ... you need only to be true.

So what's the truth inside, when you only want to hide,
If 'Be you' is what 'He' said, and go with flow just like the tide.
Now force the issue and the pain, which lies inside your head,
Or is it in wishing you weren't born, or worse still that you were dead?

Don't confuse these inner feelings, of 'is it wrong or is it right',
For life is for love and living, not being trapped within the fight.
Just remember, true love will survive ... if it is meant to be,
For no matter what will happen, eternal life-force sets you free.

So now face up to what's disguised, within the deep and hidden fear,
Wipe away from eyes and heart, those falling crystal tears.
To move on or to now stay, is the divided choice or your true goal,
To live life as one not two, have re-united souls.

David, know that love has been given to everyone and each and every living thing. Indeed, from the smallest insect to the tallest tree, to every soul, all beings, all light and to you and me.

Question 6: Why do we cry?

Answer: David, you never cease to amaze us! This question is so strange when we have 'new' information to share with you all from *across the universe. Yet, we also know why you ask this question too.*

We feel such a strong link with the last question you have asked. Is it for those who are married or who are single? Is it for the many, or for the outcast? Perhaps some who read this may think this a strange question too ... or will they?

We do not need to explain how you cry from the point of view of bodily functions. Yet the tears as they fall contain more than simple nutrients. They form part of you and your inner being. If crying is an emotion of truth, whether it is in laughter or pain, sadness or joy, then it is truly an expression that 'beholds'. It is not something to be used as a bargaining weapon or shed and given away like a 'toy'.

When 'released', your true self is given out as a physical sign of relief, laughter of love or pain. A tear can be shed and cast aside, but never from a true heart will it be in vain. A tear is a beautiful thing, beyond comprehension and it goes way beyond a simple expression.

We know that on the earth-plane you say that a smile or a picture paints a thousand words. Understand a tear does not even need a word to be spoken when you are, (or have been touched in truth), be it through a painful or joyous experience. At this moment, the well of your heart then surges and fills from within. Up and up it then rises to the top to overflow and spill and yes, it makes you 'cry'.

David, here is another poem for you to share and to know that true love is from God ... and that He really does care.

SHHH...

Shhh ... shhh, a tear so divine, it falls now from your face,
Whether alone or in a crowd, or far away in distant place.
Love is so pure, that no time or barriers can erase,
Or keep you from the light, that is forever and 'always.

So, a questions often asked, 'Oh why do we all cry?'
To release oneself a feeling ... that often goes disguised.
Whether laughter or in pain, as well as through one's love,
A tear is now expressed, as part of you from up above.

Deliverance of Love, Light and Truth

It truly is so special, and beyond any gift that you can give,
No need to ask, "Please God" ... or whether they will live.
Because as your tear does fall and you think it disappears,
You will realise you're together, so do not ever fear.

The creator is with you all, every second of your 'time',
Help nurture and understand ... your heart's connection with the mind.
For your body and your soul, and every emotion included too,
Is contained within a tear, that is made of 'Him' and you.

Thank you for the poem, it is wonderful. People may say later to me though, "Why did you not ask vastly different questions? All I can say is that I do not feel that anything else was right for this moment of time, or in fact to ask for any more answers.

This book contains so much love and guidance, and you have given so much more than I could have ever hoped for.

The Pathway and Deliverance has truly begun to help the world towards permanently join the ever-loving 'One'. I ask, please communicate again, before the commencement of last part of this book.

COMMUNICATION: *David, we thank you from our hearts that you feel the way you do. When this book is gazed upon we hope those will embrace the same feelings as you do ... and as we have discussed before, even if one-person benefits from these works or pictures then that is all that matters.*

We will begin part 3 of Endeavor when you are ready, but before we do there are a few more lines we would like to share with you which also pose a question. What you have read or learned or digested maybe different and so it may be contested. Ask yourself if it is new to you? Has this changed even the smallest part of you ... whether inside or out? Perhaps a single word may have touched your heart, or a picture has brushed against your soul's true colors. We urge you to be true to yourself and always try to reach beyond your nearest want or goal.

So, until the final piece of this book (when we shall leave you a message from beyond the Stars) re-read what has been said or simply take another look. Good-bye from us all, in peace, truth and in love and light.

Bless you always and forever. Thank you.

Saturday 14th December 1996 1.40 pm

Okay, as we now conclude these final pages I'd like to ask, "Have you learned anything? Do you think you are more spiritually aware as a person and as a soul?"

Now, as I prepare for the next communication can you say you've changed in any way? Outwardly, are you more open and honest or helpful? Are you now ready to look 'inside' to your heart and let your emotions flow so that you can grow? And, what more do you also wish to know?

Yes, there many questions I would like to ask you all but perhaps you knew these questions yourself already this day. Maybe you have even answered them 'within' yourself before you had even heard the question! Please know you are my 'brother' and my 'sister' and we form part of the eternal love and light that lives in truth.

I wish I could have a loud hailer or microphone to convey God's love to you, but I guess this book is a voice for us all. Please 'grow' and be open in your hearts. Live your life to the best of your ability and try to help others. Serve within the creator's love and light, for indeed you are divine.

I feel that today's message has now arrived to help us overcome any final fears and clear our doubts aside. I know that the Transleátions send their love to you and they always will.

COMMUNICATION: *Dear David, dear son of love and light, do not feel sad or frown and do not let your tears fall down. We are here, and we will always be within and around you all.*

So, as this chapter of this book comes to a close, know that knowledge and wisdom continue to grow. David, you saw a signal, a sign, and a shooting star last night and it was a light so bright that it lit up the night.

Likewise, it is the people who will expand their own light within and out to raise their vibration levels and their love to shout. Everyone will progress and move on to their respective 'planes' and achieve Ascension ... if they open to love and joy and peace and embrace new ways of thinking and living their lives.

An individual will experience many things and will learn more of life from a constructive viewpoint. To bridge the gap of the unknown and cross the connection to their inner self. In doing so they will open up their shell to reveal their heart's flame and find the true name that holds no blame.

When you can do this, there is no holding back unless you wish to ... free will, as always, remember? Understand that whatever faith you follow and currently believe in, grow with it if it is in the name of peace and truth. Never feel pressured into another way of life. If something is right for you it will come naturally and at the correct pace for you and those around you. Do not chastise or portion blame to others but lift their hearts if you can. A simple word or gaze into their eyes can also lift their minds and question their own purpose and manner of how and why they live their life the way they do.

We have covered much in this second book and hope it has enabled many more of you to take a look. It is now down to everyone to move forward and quicken the pace to raise the consciousness and vibration level of the human race. Every single one of you has a part to play, to grow and to move on and to save the day. To stand and deliver like the words of a song, but not with any fear, or to be threatened by the hand, knife or gun.

Many Ascended Masters wait with anticipation as the light grows across many, nations. Each fragment is growing day by day to eventually link the light's frequencies and Heaven's stairway. Today as you probably will guess, when we speak much will be said in rhyme and reason ... and this plea from our hearts is all to be true, from the young and old and every generation too.

The creator has sent messages throughout time immemorial and through many souls in more ways than you could ever imagine. These can occur through natural laws and events, or even the *mysterious 'unknown' or paranormal too ... but are these really so strange? In truth, are they all not all 'normal'?*

What we mean is that 'messages' are everyday occurrences sent via the universal light source which is God, just like the air, the wind and the rain too. Yes, from the magical illumination of the night sky to the loss of words at the so-called miracles when you ask the 'How and Why?'

There is a reference in Bible that states, "Before long, the world will not see me anymore ... but you will see me. Because I live, you also will live". Therefore, rejoice, Father/Mother God, I thank you for healing my eyes so I can see you and live". **JOHN 14:19.** *(Know that all who wish to see and believe shall do so for eternity).*

We have said many times you are all so beautiful ... as every living thing shines. You are all different vibrations yet are also one of a kind. We have asked for you to imagine your love so strong, for the strength is there for your family as well as pets and Mother Nature too. You can multiply these feelings by infinity (by what seems an impossible task) if open your hearts flame and simply ... please just ask.

You will experience love beyond comprehension ... so unique and yet the same, for you, will know and remember it deep within you. Only true love helps to erode fear, self-doubt and brings positive thought and healing and lets light 'rain' in. Deep to your core, your inner self will cry out, "Please God, may I have more." Then you may say, "Dear Savior, help me to grow in your grace, even when the tears are falling from my face." We reiterate that the creator shall wipe away all the tears from your eyes.

Remember, at the end of part two of this chapter we had stated that there was a message from beyond the stars ... this was to make the individual thirst and 'wonder'. We want you to quench your love and lights flame with an elixir that one can drink ... yet this is not one from the cup to swallow. Only through the recognition of your hearts connection can you become truly fulfilled, so do not scream or shout or holler.

This <u>will</u> quench your thirst but in another way, because it is up to you ... so consider your yesterday and your today. It is simple then this message from our hearts, that we are one with you

Deliverance of Love, Light and Truth

and the light and will never ever part.

You might be expecting us to say something extraordinary to you now. Maybe it will be? Or, you might have known it all along? We hope you will now take time to reflect upon what is shared, and decide on the route you next take, and the decisions you may face. Please decide whether this book is fact or fiction on your shelf, and if the door is wide open to your one true self. Know too ...this will not be relayed to you as a question, but in the 'words' of a poem ... called Choice.

CHOICE

You have always had a choice and the free will to move on,
And there are decisions to be made, but no push me-pull you along.
You are so unique, and are made of beautiful light,
To shine like brilliant stars, within the deepest, darkest night.

One day when 'time' is right, then you will understand,
You are born of such brilliance ... from a guiding loving hand.
So now acknowledge what you are, the inner you and God's pure love,
Eternally delivered ... a gift of light within and up above.

Please decide to express your 'self' ... and to learn once more again,
Of that of what is with you, to be expanded and retrain.
Or you might have just forgotten, of how to just exist,
Blinded by non-reality, the material ... are you clouded in the mist?

So, blow out negativity, that has bound and binds you so,
And clearly, you'll discover, that new seeds can then be sown.
These rays of light vibrations, are so rare like divine gold,
A discovery for all eternity, you never can grow old.

Yes, everything is then born, of the creator's brilliant hand,
And we are all no different, no matter what planet, nation, or land.
So, whatever is your tongue or the color of your skin...
You can truly live-in peace, and forever without sin.

Endeavor

So, rejoice and lift your heart, to the everlasting sun,
And meet and walk the truth, on a journey with the Son.
Many Ascended Masters, and those angels are true friends,
Will guide you where you need, for their love is without end.

But the truth and all those choices ... are yours alone to make,
And now you learn this too, about what really is at stake.
Your live(s) are but a glimpse, a small fragment of light not time,
A chance to grow then know, of the love and truth 'divine'.

So, now this message ends, and we hope you'll go to 'Him'.
To the one eternal home and another new beginning.
For this most beautiful peace, is more than imagination,
It is for each and every soul ... so now share with every nation.

David, it is time for us to take flight, but we have left a few lines spare for you to conclude from your heart, just as you did before. Be true my son and never doubt your abilities to sow and to serve, for everyone has their job and place to grow.

Please continue to open your heart to the 'divine' ... and for those who read or listen to this book, forever be in love, light, and truth from us all. Remember,

You can then all be, what you only can become,
Part of the eternal source, the all-loving 'one'.
Love and light be with you, always and together...
As you are all of light, and of a love that lasts forever.

Goodbye (for now), from Millanderer and all the Trans-leátions of the Two Sisters Star Group.

Dear, dear Trans-leátions thank you from my heart ... for all the words of love that have flowed through this pen. I know it will pour forth again when it is ready to do so, but until then, I hope and I pray that we can all grow together, forever. Goodbye for now.

Sunday 8th February 1997

It seems so long ago, almost two months now, but it was as if I knew within myself that one last communication was to be delivered and would now come through.

COMMUNICATION: *Hello David. The pen is of the light, the source of truth and peace. It flows through all of thee. Much has been learned and forsaken by the individual and perhaps across many nations. Now it is time to re-connect, the time to grow and move on to really know who you are and what you are here for. Indeed, the answers to why were you born and why your body dies ... these are questions that burn within the heart ... and also make you cry.*

So, it is time to face yourself or leave the truth unknown. Do you wish to begin the lines of communication again ... like the ringing of the phone? And, has your heart now skipped a beat to leave you feeling buoyant, afloat, but with thoughts that you're alone? Gaze over your shoulder by all means, for you are not drifting upon a cold forgotten sea or track ... just overcome all doubt in the knowledge there is no need to ever look back.

Know that a new page has begun and with it is the choice to relive anew what you had already thought was fun. Perhaps you will change your thoughts again and those true wishes, your desire to learn and express, maybe even move to a new address? Appreciate we are always close by in love and light too, and we will never forget or be far away from you. Dear Lord Jesus is also with you always and that is no less a fact, for He is so beautiful and His strength in you will never lack. We are all one and this shall remain so into eternity.

When we came, you had 'shown' us a door ... a simple request to reveal some more. The dream you had recently received was a message. You had been feeling alone and searched for new work to be 'done' for a while. But this is to quench your thirst, for you to be still and make you think ... yes the light and peace for you to breathe and also drink.

You have learned this many times before, (and from other guides) to simply turn within. Have you forgotten what it's like to be still and free from 'din'? You all need to grow but you cannot be quiet (to remove yourself from the senses) when you are actively pushed and pulled in other directions.

David, this is just a brief message before our new task is set. It is a reminder if you like, my son. Please strive towards the light. We have another poem for you all and we hope you can re-connect with these new words.

"RE-CONNECTION"

Two sparks ignite the light, bringing darkness back to day.
And even when you think you're lost, the truth will pave the way.
Your growth and illumination, both start from deep within,
When individuals connect their flame ... of love and light, not sin.

A burst, a flash, the inspiration ... perhaps in words or of a song,
Sweet memories of one God, all back where we belong.
Such movement and emotions ...tears falling from your hearts,
To know we're one together, from the beginning we will not part.

Both born and twice evolved, from the creator, the divine,
The light it does not say, of what is yours or what is mine.
But it shares and also gives, free love to hearts and minds,
For you to do your best ... don't pretend your soul is blind.

So hence this new addition, to illuminate once again,
Truth is from the 'source' ... through words written by this pen.
To be seen or may be heard, by one or by the many,
For reflections of your soul, are not communications from the telly.

Please come and then fulfill, your individual and group goal,
To ascend the eternal hill, the true plane of all joined souls.
So now be still and ready, for eyes not opened can be deceived,
But with your heart both pure and open, you'll succeed your own true needs.

Deliverance of Love, Light and Truth

Enough for now David, as it is your free will to proceed again when the time is right for you. Yes, your choice and your Pathway remain on a continuous golden bridge which lays before you. Remember to always learn and forgive and to serve. Goodbye, my son, for now.

Thank you once again dear Trans-leátions, for all that you have shared with me. I will never forget your love and peace and all the guidance you have shared with me and also for the many too. May Love, light and truth be always and forever in your hearts.

P.S. To all who read this book, I would like to share the following decree so that you. May keep it safe and always in your heart. May God bless you all. Goodbye and good luck.

Endeavor

HOLY CHRIST FLAME

Thou Holy Christ Flame within my heart,
Help me to manifest all thou art.
Teach me to see thyself in all,
Help me to show men how to call.

All of thy glory from the Sun,
'Till earth's great victory is won.
I AM we love thee, thou art our all!
I AM, we love thee, hear our call!

I hear thy call, my children dear,
I AM thy heart, so never fear.
I AM your mind, your body, too,
I AM in every cell of you.

I AM thy earth and sea and sky,
And not one soul shall I pass by.
I AM in thee; thou art in me,
I AM, I AM thy victory.

ENDNOTES

1. Pathway: Channelled text (Book 1) from the Trans-leátions.

2. Trans-leátions: Light 'Beings' who reside 1000 Light Years from Earth.

3. Pleiades: This Star constellation is known as the 7 Sisters Star Group or its modern term, M45.

4. Colors: Green and purple, (for healing and psychic abilities) which seemed like magnets that attracted me ... perhaps they would be colors for the book cover too?

5. Two sisters' symbol: Where an image of a man becomes identical to a woman who is close by him, as if they were 'twins'– 'Two Sisters!'

6. Milanderer and Zerrog: Two of the Trans-leátions.

7. Sheila: A special friend and colleague who typed the Pathway manuscript for me.

8. Little improvement: I had this immense feeling that they meant the recent terrorist bombings and the struggle for global peace.

9. Planes: The innumerable dimensions of consciousness of light.

10. Fifth Dimension: A higher plane of consciousness, celestial heaven.

11. Clairaudience: Clear 'hearing' of messages from the 'spirit' world and planes of consciousness.

12. Heart's flame: This is your soul's Three-Fold Flame that is seated in the center of your heart.

13. Ascensions: I.E ... after the 4th and final 'wave' of ascension to the 'New' home made for all of Creation.

14. Dunblane: The children and their teacher who were murdered at school in the Scottish town of Dunblane.

15. Manila: A fire in a discotheque that killed many people.

16. Regression: It revealed to me that I was a lady in the Victorian 'era', who had survived by living a life of easy virtue! This sounds quite alarming, but I ask, "How can you learn what you need in just one lifetime? How different would your experiences be if you were born with a different color skin, if you were rich or poor, or if you were the opposite sex?

17. Workshop: A group attended by 15 people, which had been held at Lizzy's. She is a crystal healer and friend. We had learned new affirmations, prayers and much more about the incarnations of St Germain and the Violet Flame.

18. Ascended Masters: Jesus, St Germain, and many more.

19. Self and Higher Self: Self can represent the little or 'ego' self. The Higher Self is the Christ consciousness (the all-knowing), the witness self or the watcher within.

20. Decrees: These are 'mantras'–a word or formula and they attune and govern a release of energy. They cleanse and clear karma and are also a command to 'ordain'.

21. Summit Lighthouse University: Organized by Elizabeth (c)

Endnotes

Prophet in America.

22. Millanderer: The first 'light' being of the Trans-leátions to contact me.

23. Karma: Many already know, this is the record of all discord which the individual has generated not only in this lifetime but also throughout all embodiments long past.

24. Hypnologic Imagery: Just before we wake up or also fall asleep, our minds can be in a strange state of consciousness. During this, we can sometimes see images or experience sensations that do seem real.

25. Temporal Lobe Liability: Areas of the brain are linked with emotion, memory, and the understanding of speech and these are called Temporal Lobes. They can be unstable and are responsive to stimulation and may give rise to someone feeling a strange presence, panic or also ascending in the air.

26. Statement: In a recent meditation I learnt that Jesus would come to tell me something in a dream. Later that night, I had experienced an amazing vision of him ... he stood before me and the brightness of his 'being' was so immense, it blurred my sight of him. Yet inside of me, I knew it was Jesus, for he spoke through 'His' heart to mine. Wonderful!

27. Elohim: A plural noun. These twin flames are the builders of form that is the entire matter Universe, including us. The Elohim (with 7 'Rays') are represented by Archangels and Ascended Masters.

28. Divine 'Spark: This is made up of the Blue (will) of God (Father/Mother), the Yellow–(wisdom) of God (Son) and the Pink–(love) of God ... hence the Holy Spirit– 'THE TRINITY'.

29. Ray of Light: All three flames 'become' ONE, for each are all blue, then yellow, then pink, before turning the Ascension 'white'. (As the vibration level and rate increases the color will then change ... for they all go to white. Hence, this is the white 'Ascension Ray').

30. Physical Learning Plane: It is a Soul's own free will and choice to return to the Earth plane to progress and learn. The Soul has never been forced to do so by God.

31. White: The White Light of Love and Creation, not 'race'. It is a reference to the 'AURA' of white light that surrounds the 'Immortals'.

32. Brotherhood: Hierarchy of 'Beings' that include the Ascended Master ... a Spiritual 'order' of Western saints and Eastern masters (Brothers and Sisters) who have graduated from earth's schoolroom and who have Ascended.

33. Ascension Waves: As mentioned in 'Pathway', these are points in 'time' when the individuals and masses link to the Ascension cords of Light.

34. Elementals: Of Fire, Air, Water and Earth. These are the life 'forces' that exist in each of these elements.

35. Inner Silver Cord: The silver or crystal cord is the life force energy or stream of life. It comes from God, our creator's heart to our higher consciousness/or Christ 'self' to energize, feed and sustain you and your soul as well as its expressions and bodies of time and space. This is achieved through the linking of your chakras (energy points). You could say the cord is an umbilical cord of life and it is through this cord that God's love and energy flows through your 'transpersonal' chakras and into your crown. This is your heartbeat of the physical heart and of your soul's Three-Fold Flame.

Endnotes

36. The lower self: Consists of the soul evolving through the four planes of matter using the vehicle of the four lower bodies, (I.E, the Etheric or Astral, mental, emotional, and physical body), both to balance Karma and fulfill the 'divine plan'.

37. Pink: Also known as the 3rd Ray- The love of God and representative of the Heart chakra.

38. Yellow: the 2nd Ray for the wisdom and illumination of God and representative via the crown chakra.

39. Son: Can also be deemed as the Universal Christ 'Light' within everything.

40. Green: (Including Emerald Green). This is the 5th Ray, of Truth and Healing. It is representative of precipitation with the 'mind's eye' or 3rd chakra.

41. Blue: This is the 1st Ray and is the will/power of God. Therefore, we call the plans of things a 'blue' print. It is representative of the throat chakra.

42. Indigo: This is the 6th Ray; it is representative of 'Service and Ministration'.

43. Slashed: I had recently contacted the local police. Two of my car tires (and some neighbors' vehicles too) had been punctured with a knife.

44. Violet: The 7th Ray. This is representative of Transmutation, Ritual and Alchemy. 45 Bodies: Etheric /Astral, Physical, Mental and Emotional.

45. Life: International News story: LIFE ON MARS. How a piece of 'rock' discovered on Earth was said to have fallen from Mars and how the world's scientists reported their analysis.

46. Earthly Home: At the time I took this to mean the mental, emotional, etheric, or astral as well as the physical body.

47. Animal: NB: About six months later (April 1997) I saw an article in a newspaper (The Daily Mail) regarding 'Alien visitations and the most popular appearances witnessed by humankind. One sketch and description were remarkably like the 'being' I had met. The name had been given to these 'beings', ANIMALANS!

48. Stellar Gateway Chakra: A 'cosmic' energy point, which is an inlet and outlet that's approximately 18" above the head.

49. Akashic Records: The Universal learning center for all life and light. All knowledge and wisdom that is past, present, and future and everything that ever was, is, and shall be ... are written here.

ABOUT THE AUTHOR

David has helped to conduct spiritual development and healing circles for over 25 years. He has also been a guest speaker—sharing his enlightened experiences to promote 'oneness'—at various Mind, Body and Spirit engagements across the UK. Through inner-dictation, dream interpretation, meditation, mindfulness, pre-cognition, and healing, the books he co-writes with 'Spirit' provide you with the foundation to discover your own path of truth. With a renewed sense of purpose, the spiritual guidance and education you receive can help you reach the goal of self-realization and bliss within the permanence of love and light. David is tee-total and a vegetarian, who loves the sunshine, nature, animals, and his wife!

INVITATION FROM DAVID KNIGHT

Join David's mission for a 'full and blissful life' at
https://www.ascensionforyou.com

Follow us on Facebook facebook.com/ascensionforyou
or Twitter https://twitter.com/ascensionforyou

and become part of our community who love to receive uplifting messages for the heart and Soul!

Want to let others know what you think? Please make your opinion known by leaving a 'star rating' with one-click on Amazon.com or Amazon.co.uk and /or a review at your favourite online retailer.
Thank you!

www.ingramcontent.com/pod-product-compliance
Lightning Source LLC
LaVergne TN
LVHW021705060526
838200LV00050B/2509